Lloyd on Lloyd

Carol Thatcher studied law at London University and qualified as a solicitor then spent five years in Australia where she worked on a Northern Territory cattle station and New South Wales thoroughbred stud farm before turning to a journalistic career. She spent two years as a reporter on the *Sydney Morning Herald*, including six months covering proceedings in Parliament House, Canberra, then became a TV reporter and interviewer on a Sydney current affairs programme. In 1981 she returned to Britain where she worked as a freelance journalist and presented a radio phone-in show, joining the staff of the *Daily Telegraph* in 1982. *Lloyd on Lloyd* is her second book; her first was *Diary of an Election*, an account of Margaret Thatcher's 1983 election campaign.

CHRIS and JOHN LLOYD with CAROL THATCHER

Lloyd ON Lloyd

Fontana/Collins

First published by Willow Books 1985
First issued in Fontana Paperbacks 1986

Copyright © Evert Enterprises Inc. and John Lloyd 1985

Made and printed in Great Britain by
William Collins Sons & Co. Ltd, Glasgow

To Both Our Families

Contents

Preface

This is both a tennis book, and a biography. It is John and Chris Lloyd's story of twelve years on the international tennis circuit, six of them as husband and wife.

Just as the rich are not like the rest of us, so also we believe that the marriages of the famous are different. The backstage lives of stars – whether they're actors, sports personalities or politicians – seem to be glittering and larger than life, the figment of our dreams. What I have tried to capture from John and Chris is an impression of the training and the tension, the practice and the performance at the pinnacle of international tennis, and how they combine these demands with marriage when home is a hotel suite and work entails an inter-continental flight every other week, frequently in opposite directions from each other.

The glamorous image of tennis megastars enjoying perpetual partying is mythical in the Lloyds's case. During one of the Grand Slam tournaments – Wimbledon and the French, US and Australian Opens – Chris is more likely to be found eating a room-service dinner while studying a video of her next day's opponent or relaxing in front of the television than bopping in the trendiest disco in town. When she won her sixteenth Grand Slam title at the

Australian Open in Melbourne in 1984, it was only because an airline dispute had stranded them there that John and Chris managed to have a celebration dinner together after the final. Otherwise they would have flown straight up to Sydney to get settled into another hotel so John could prepare for his tournament the following week, with Chris switching from the role of champion to that of Mrs J. M. Lloyd, supporting her husband.

During the thousands of miles of travel which the Lloyds chalk up each year, the main sensation they get is jetlag. They are frequently oblivious of their surroundings, and have few of the pleasurable experiences associated with the jet-set life. Top tennis players can fly to a country, check in to their hotel, play, win or lose and leave without so much as having to change their travellers' cheques into the local currency, let alone hearing the native tongue, such is the insulated routine of tournament courtesy cars to press conferences, courts, locker rooms and back to hotels.

Apart from Billie Jean King in a different era Chris's career has been a unique and an enduring one – from that of a teenage prodigy who became an overnight sensation at the 1971 US Open, to the world's almost unbeatable no. 1 for five consecutive years, to a no. 2 who is constantly challenging the present no. 1 Martina Navratilova. She was the original teenager who created the tennis boom, inspiring a spate of young players, few of whom have been able to sustain their success while remarkably Chris plays on. She has paced herself, and durability has been the dividend: in December 1984 she notched up her 1000th win in Melbourne.

John has had no ordinary career either. Ranked no. 24 in the world in 1978, he nosedived into the three hundreds and spent several years in oblivion. He clawed his way back to no. 77 by the end of 1983 and a year later was back in the no. 24 position – a commendable achievement except in the eyes of those who contend that if he had worked harder earlier, he could have been ranked even higher.

I arrived in Melbourne on 4 December, 1984 to start work with John and Chris on *Lloyd on Lloyd* which had to be completed by 28 February, 1985. This inelastic deadline meant that the book was both researched and written on the run. John and Chris found themselves talking into my tape recorder by practice courts, in hotel rooms, in cars, on planes and at home in Palm Springs, California and Fort Lauderdale, Florida. I thank them sincerely for their conscientious attention, candid answers and for the pleasure of working with them. Similar thanks are owed to Jimmy and Colette Evert and Denis and Doris Lloyd for inviting me to their homes. I have tried to ensure that all the facts and figures in the book are accurate, but must emphasize that the responsibility for any mistakes is mine alone.

I would like to express my gratitude to all the people round the world who helped me and were so generous with their time, and would like to mention Winn Carr, Woman's Page editor of the *Daily Telegraph*, for allowing me time off at short notice.

Most of all I am deeply indebted to Sally Louis who toiled with great efficiency to put the manuscript on a word processor, amending it whenever necessary. Special thanks to Ingrid Bentzer for a fund of stories told in her inimitable lively way, and to my editor, Caroline White.

Towards the end, when the deadline began to look impossible, I had no better example of how to achieve an objective single-mindedly than that of the thoroughly admirable Chris Lloyd.

Carol Thatcher
February 1985

CHAPTER ONE

Different Players, Different People

John Lloyd had never played better tennis. In the blazing September sun he gave what was quite simply a virtuoso performance against 7th seed Johan Kriek, the Florida-based South African, in the third round of the 1984 US Open at Flushing Meadow.

This was how John's fans, coach and wife had longed to see him play for the past five years, but they had frequently despaired of him ever doing so as time after time his lack of tenacity had let down his undoubted on-court flair.

The 20,000 capacity Stadium Court was so packed that the gates had been shut long before and the atmosphere was electric. In the eyes of the brazen New York crowd John was not only the much liked, good-looking husband of their favourite star, Chris Evert (whom many of the crowd had watched grow from teenage prodigy to an admired and respected sportswoman), but also the underdog, and therefore to be sided with.

In a previous match against Peter Fleming – and in the 1983 US Open when he'd reached the last sixteen – John had shown that he could play superb tennis and cause the unexpected exits of top seeds. Now the crowd was excitedly willing him on, anticipating a thrilling match against Kriek and another, all too rare, Lloyd victory.

In the first game Kriek hit three cannonballing aces, followed by so many other guaranteed winners in that set, which he won 6–2, that it looked as though he would defeat John as the form predicted. 'I wouldn't have been surprised if the result was 6–2, 6–3, 6–2,' John Barrett, who was commentating for BBC Television, thought to himself up in the commentary box.

But a changed John Lloyd, with a new-found will to win, hung on and took control in the second set at a crucial time when he admits that in years gone by he would have just given up and resigned himself to defeat.

In the stands, agonizing over her husband's every shot, sat Chris, the tennis superstar John had married in a glamorous white wedding in 1979. At the time their love story seemed to have been set in a sort of fantasy land dreamed up by the media, and the marriage of the game's golden couple had been elevated to a fabulous partnership. Britain's no. 2 – as John was then – and the world's no. 1 woman player had been expected to walk down the aisle and live happily ever after, winning on court and enjoying a charmed existence off it.

Within two years, however, the fairytale had lost its magic, and wealth and success couldn't render them immune to normal marital problems. These had eventually led to a six-month separation, and they had only been happily reconciled weeks before the US Open in 1984.

That afternoon while John was on court playing his best, Mrs Lloyd took on the role of tennis wife rather than no. 2 player in the world, following every shot her husband hit with the same intense concentration she would if she'd been wielding the racket herself. Occasionally she'd murmur, 'Let's go John,' 'Come on John,' 'Great shot,' as if talking to him by remote control. She sometimes chewed gum with an exorcising vigour to lessen the tension which visibly racked her. Her face wore a pained expression, and she perpetually crossed and uncrossed her legs.

At the end of the first set John and Kriek were in a tense tie-breaker which had Chris on the edge of her seat. 'It was so dramatic; it was draining to watch,' she remembered. One minute John was in a winning position and Chris would start to relax, then a change of fortunes would put Kriek in front and she would brace herself, every muscle taut, sighing an audible, 'Oh no.'

John recovered from trailing 3–1 down in the tie-breaker to have two set points at 6–5 and 8–7 which, taxing Chris's nerves mercilessly, he let slip away. At 9–8, he took his eye off the ball – a momentary loss of concentration which can be fatal – but miraculously luck was on his side and his miscued smash just clipped the line. It was in, making it John's set and one set-all; he was back in business and it was anyone's match.

Chris breathed out as did Bob Brett, John's young Australian coach who had learned some of his coaching skills from the legendary Australian Davis Cup mastermind, Harry Hopman. Ironically he had once also helped Kriek, John's opponent now, with his game. Bob was sitting by himself, by choice, because it enabled him to concentrate better on the match – far from the sighs of relief, groans of disappointment and nervous chatter of John and Chris's party of friends and relations.

What they were all seeing was more than just the renaissance of a tennis player; it was the transformation of the character of Chris's husband, too. Gone was the old John who'd been so prone to bouts of compulsive losing because he just wouldn't try, a fault which was totally incomprehensible to Chris, whose success was based on sheer hard slog and a strong competitiveness. What had irked her so often during their married life was John's lack of singlemindedness and drive.

'It didn't surprise me how well John was playing; I always knew he had it in him. What made me proudest was that he'd made a commitment to his tennis. The shots were always there, it was just the mental strength he'd lacked. Even when Kriek hit sizzling passing shots John tried, and I hadn't seen a lot of that in five years.'

What she had seen in that time were countless incidents of John literally chucking away matches when not only his will to win had suddenly evaporated but also his basic desire to compete had deserted him. For a player like Chris, whose hallmarks were chalking up record streaks of match wins and pulling victory from the jaws of defeat when an occasion demanded it, it had been intolerable. As she watched John battle to victory, she fervently hoped these incidents were now history.

Four years earlier, at the same venue where she was now sitting proudly watching her husband, she had walked out of one of his matches, disgusted and in tears. John had been beating American college student Leif Shiras when suddenly he had lost all his energy and his will to win and just gave up. Consumed by a feeling of fatalism, he had been defeated.

Just after they were married in 1979 she had watched with despair at the Italian Open in Rome as John threw away a great lead over Australian Phil Dent after he'd hit just one bad shot. John had magnified the loss of this point into a great catastrophe and consequently had lost the next twelve games in a row. The new bride, in tears, had told him he had no guts and pleaded with him to give one hundred per cent to whatever he did, whether it was tennis or painting walls. Now she watched the Kriek match with growing pride as John survived breaks of serve in the third and fourth sets and continued playing magnificent tennis to win the match 2–6, 7–6, 6–2, 6–3.

He shook hands with Kriek at the net to an ecstatic reception from the vociferous New York crowd who had appreciated the standard of the tennis and John's subtle tactical handling of Kriek. It was a very popular win for this easy-going Englishman. Chris wiped away the tears of pride and rushed proudly to congratulate her husband.

Although John wins about as rarely as Chris loses, no one rejoices more in his victories than she does. She always publicly heaps credit on him and when he loses narrowly, as opposed to giving up, defends him against the cynics and critics who are only too quick to say 'Lloyd crashes' rather than acknowledge that he'd played creditably against an opponent who was simply too good. It was irrelevant to her that John's victory over Kriek was just a third round win when she had only once in eleven years lost in a Grand Slam event before the semi-finals.

After the match Bob Brett, who later singled out John's performance in this match as a highlight of his own coaching career, went to wait for John in the locker room, brimming with satisfaction at the way his client had played.

John's tennis in that match won him unanimous praise, not least of all from his defeated opponent who could only marvel at the new standard of John's game. 'I don't see why he shouldn't climb into the top ten or fifteen in the world, the way he was playing today. He was awesome,' Kriek said. John rated it among his best matches, and confidence flowed from him where there had been none in the past years. Everything had clicked.

British newspapers, so starved of successful events to report on the tennis front, trumpeted John's victory, too, and some even went as far as to talk about a new optimism for the country's tennis. All over the world, from the United States where the match had taken place, to Britain, to Spain, where John had been coached as a teenager at Lew Hoad's Campo de Tenis, and where Lew welcomed the news of John's victory with cheery excitement, people were congratulating John on his success.

While he hadn't earned himself a place in the record books (of which his wife can boast many), nevertheless it was a small mention for a British player in the history of the US Open and, more importantly, a phenomenal personal achievement at long last. The victory was doubly special because in many senses it was a vindication of the Lloyds's decision to get back together again. Here, for Chris, was a man who did after all have the will to win.

The match for her had been a totally exhausting experience even though she hadn't swung a racket. For a professional, watching a match being played by someone you are involved with consumes nervous energy and is thoroughly draining. Often Chris feels as though she hasn't slept for a week after enduring one of John's fraught and drama-packed marathon matches. She has even had migraines in reaction to the stress.

She isn't the only tennis spouse who has found the business of spectating almost unbearable. Ilie Nastase's ex-wife, Dominique, once said, 'I feel everything he feels out there. I understand so well what he goes through. I die when I see him play sometimes.'

Over the years Chris has teased John about how much easier a time he has watching her than the other way round, if only because his long matches protract the agony: 'Why do you have to make it so dramatic? At least I win 6–2, 6–1!'

'I could never be a full-time "tennis wife"; it's too tough,' she's often declared. Nor is she just a part-time 'tennis wife' either – she's the no. 2 in the world, three times Wimbledon victor, six times US Open champion and in 1984 she passed her 1000th singles win.

When she does watch John, she has to mitigate the damage done by the strain of spectating before she plays her own matches often later the same day or the following one.

Experts such as the Lloyds's Melbourne physiotherapist, Stan Nicholes, lecture their athletes that if they go out and lie in the sun before a match they may as well forget their match because the loss of body fluids is tiring both mentally and physically. John and Chris go through a similar strain when they sit in stands in the full glare of the blazing sun, trembling, sweating and tense as they watch one another on court, and potentially jeopardizing their own chances in subsequent matches. Both agree that watching each other is far worse than actually playing and try to compromise whenever possible by sitting in the shade.

'The US Open was a real test because John had so many close matches but I sat through them all,' Chris said after the tournament. 'I went through a lot of nervous tension but I wouldn't have missed them for anything in the world. I made up my mind to do my practising before his match because I knew I wouldn't be fit for anything afterwards. I watched each match, then afterwards we went back to the hotel together and relaxed. We do have an unwritten rule that if we both play on the same day the one who plays second watches one set of four or five games and then goes back to the locker room because it's just not worth it otherwise.'

Home for the fortnight of the US Open was a flat in the St Moritz Hotel on Central Park and Fifth Avenue. They'd flown over Jenny Scally, who cooks for them at their Kingston home during Wimbledon, which ensured that John had copious quantities of treacle tart and hot custard which had been his favourite fare from Southend schooldays. The amount he gets through is a standing joke in the Lloyd household. Although it is more suited to a cold English winter than the simulated cool of New York provided by the air-conditioning on an otherwise hot, steamy, Manhattan evening, Jenny had arrived laden with tins of golden syrup and packets of custard powder prepared for the task.

After his triumph over Kriek John's next opponent was ninth seed, Sweden's Henrik Sundstrom, for a place in the quarter-finals. The match was a trial of epic proportions for both Lloyds. It started at eleven o'clock in the morning, and because of two interruptions caused by rain, didn't finish until the early evening under lights with John the 4–6, 6–4, 6–4, 6–2 victor.

During one of the downpours, John suggested to Chris that, since she had to play Sylvia Hanika of West Germany the following day in the quarter-finals, she shouldn't sit through the entire match. But unselfishly she had no doubts and knew she had to be there. 'There was no question in my mind as to what I should do. I had decided that to go out the next day after John's match thinking how tired I was would be bad so I tried instead to go out thinking positively, "Well, that was yesterday; I've had a good night's sleep and this is a new day so it shouldn't make any difference."' She made sure that it didn't and beat Sylvia Hanika easily enough with a score of 6–2, 6–3.

John's quarter-final against defending champion Jimmy Connors, who had once been engaged to Chris, wasn't going to be nearly so easy. John had never beaten him and three years before at the US Open Connors had humiliated him 6–0, 6–0, 6–2.

Whatever the result was to be John had already acquitted himself admirably in the 1984 US Open. His track record until then showed that his standard of play on any given day – however positive the indicators – was always a gamble, and his recovery had been very erratic right until Flushing Meadow. The final breakthrough had come in the previous tournament, the ATP Championships in Cincinnati. He had been very much into his old ways of not fighting hard enough to win a winnable match and had lost 7–5, 6–1 to young Swede, Stefan Edberg. Bob Brett had been livid. He had employed methods ranging from gentle encouragement to firm talks to get his message across and now contained his fury only until they reached the car park, where he exploded. 'You never thought you were going to win; you gave up,' he said. 'No, I didn't give up,' defended John, gesturing to Bob to lower his voice, rather embarrassed at this public dressing-down in the presence of other players, but Bob was only just beginning.

'It was a pathetic performance. How do you expect to get to the top again if you don't think you can beat people like that? The match was there for the taking. You could have won it, but you just gave it to him.'

'I almost told him to get lost,' John remembered, 'because I wasn't paying him to abuse me, but basically I knew he was right.' The grilling over, Bob stalked off in disgust to play golf but his words had the desired effect. They finally instilled in John what his wife had never been able to convey to him. Even her example hadn't ever inspired him to compete to the end of every match.

The beginning of John's astounding recovery lay nine months earlier in the Lloyds's dramatic separation, which had been at Chris's suggestion. Their marriage had hit the rocks – the first brutal thing that had happened to John in the charmed life he had led from being a junior champion, to the golden hero of Wimbledon at twenty-two, to his marriage to the world's no. 1 tennis star. It was this emotional catastrophe which had been largely responsible for John finally beginning to knuckle under and make a serious effort to resurrect his game.

During that separation Chris saw him submerging all his passion and emotion into his game. John viewed his effort as the more constructive of two alternatives: 'I realized that I could sit around all day moping and calling Chris up, pleading with her to come back, or I could carry on as I'd already started – dedicatedly and consistently working on my game and training hard.' Whereas it was separation which had motivated John into getting his game up to scratch, he credited the happiness and harmony which reconciliation had brought for his winning performances at the US Open. 'From a purely practical point of view, if Chris and I had still been separated then, we'd have been staying in different hotels, only talking on the telephone and avoiding being seen together because the press would have been chasing us. If that had been the case, I doubt very much whether I would even have reached the quarterfinals,' he said.

It had been tough for John and Chris to separate, to publicly announce that the reality was different from the image; that the gleaming halos which the public had placed over the heads of its hallowed tennis couple had slipped. Concern about tarnish on their image and the sniping they would be open to was one of the reasons the Lloyds had delayed actually separating for a year. In fact, it would probably have been more surprising had they managed to make two tennis careers flourish *and* a marriage succeed.

The failure rate of couples who had tried to combine marriage and life on the circuit was high – even when only one of them was a player. Mariana Simionescu, a Romanian professional who had been ranked no. 37 in the world, quit when she married Bjorn Borg, but even devoting herself to being a full-time tennis wife didn't prevent them getting divorced in Monte Carlo in 1984.

Jimmy Connors married his ex-Playboy girl and model, Patti, six months before Chris and John's wedding but they'd had problems and separated too for a long period. It was well nigh impossible for a husband and wife who were both players, and even harder in the Lloyds's case. 'We're different as players and people, with different temperaments and styles,' Chris herself said. A whirlwind court-ship of three dates during Wimbledon in 1978 followed by snatched weekends and weeks in hotels on two continents meant that two twenty-four-year-olds who were very much in love, but who didn't know each other very well, walked down the aisle on 17 April, 1979 with a 'love conquers all' approach to marriage.

Love never does, of course, and particularly not when the men's and women's tennis circuits have separated to the extent that practically the only tournaments where they were playing together were the four Grand Slam events – Wimbledon, the French, US and Australian Opens. These took up eight weeks a year, fraught, in the Lloyds's case, with the strains of winning or losing, concentrating on their own careers and supporting each other. For the rest of the year they were playing at different tournaments, often thousands of miles apart.

Regular married life for the Lloyds settled down to an artificial round of hotel suites, room service, tournament courtesy cars to the practice courts, matches and press conferences. Apart from eating out in the occasional restaurant they often had little idea whether it was Collins Street, Melbourne or the Champs Elysée, Paris beyond the hotel foyer.

Chris and John both regard hotels as home and they're now so used to the noise coming up from the kitchens, the disco, other guests or the main road outside that they have difficulty sleeping in the quiet of their Kingston home in a peaceful Surrey backwater. When they are at different tournaments they talk frequently on the telephone but that is never ideal with the time differences and one winning, the other losing. While in Rome for playing in the Davis Cup tournament in 1979, John spent hours on the phone at two and three o'clock in the morning to Chris (who was competing in the US Open in New York) which did nothing for his performance. Then there is the friction: 'Why didn't you phone?' 'I didn't want to wake you up.' 'But I was expecting a call; you could have woken me up to reassure me you'd got in all right or to tell me the result.'

Their lives are rarely what could be called normal, not because of the fabled hedonistic lifestyle of the tennis circuit, but because of the unceasing grind of staying mentally and physically competitive and the monotony of being on the road.

' "Normal" people take the bus to their office, but tennis players take the plane, due to the inconvenience of "the office" being moved all over the world. It seems like an enviable lifestyle – people read about us jetting off to London, to Paris, to Rome via LA and Hawaii but the truth is we get a lot of jetlag and we're training hard and playing once we're at tournaments. We don't have time to go out sightseeing or to the nightspots a lot. If we're not working out or playing we're on a plane, on our way to the next match. Every year we have six or eight weeks off when we can lie in the sun at our house in Palm Springs. Apart from those luxurious weeks it's hard work,' Chris and John agreed.

The marriage, which from the outside looking in seemed such a stylish and idyllic liaison between two good looking, permanently tanned, talented tennis stars, couldn't help but be complicated and strained by their opposite traits on and off court.

Chris is two contrasting personalities. With a racket in her hand she is the champion who wills her way to victory ruthlessly, with a steely determination even when her shots are less than perfect. But off court she is charming, warm, amusing, affectionate and considerate. She turns up at the courts for a Grand Slam final riddled with nerves. oblivious to everything but the match, though her thoughtfulness is shown by little things such as her still remembering to bring with her a bottle of borrowed nail polish remover to return to the lender.

When waving off an English friend in a taxi outside her parents' front door in Fort Lauderdale, she is pragmatic and considerate enough to call out: 'Have you got any American money?'

The first thing she did when Kathy Jordan so unexpectedly defeated her at Wimbledon in 1983 – though she was sick and overcome with despair and disappointment – was to telephone her cook, knowing that television commentators had been speculating about the cause of her stomach upset and that the cook would be very worried and mistakenly blaming herself.

John is the same mild-mannered, pleasant individual on and offcourt. Though competitive when he wants to be, he admits that he isn't imbued with his wife's burning passion to win. Chris analysed his philosophy. 'I think John's worried that he's going to turn into a bad guy if he reaches the heights of a tennis career. I've tried to tell him that you can be selfish on court and still be nice off it; that there is a time and place for everything.'

Chris is the motivator with a strong discipline and a sense of priorities. In their Palm Springs home she will flip through the *Yellow Pages* to find the number of the video store to call up and ask what time they shut, because John has lain by the pool all afternoon instead of taking the video in for repair.

John is an attractive player whose in-built flair tempts him to go for the flashy shot which, if it comes off is a spectacular winner, but if it doesn't is an outright loser – the Russian roulette approach. Chris doggedly, with bull's-eye accuracy, slugs out long rallies from the baseline, interminably if necessary because her father had instilled into her as a child that 'the player who makes the least errors wins the match'.

One was a man who was simply satisfied with modest wins: 'I was quite happy getting through the qualifying matches and winning a round here and there.' while his wife barely dares pause to enjoy another Grand Slam victory before fixing her sights on the next tournament.

'I have always been single-minded. It's almost as if I had a fear that if I really had fun it would distract me and detract from my tennis. I was afraid someone might come and take my success away if I started patting myself on the back and dwelling on my victories too much,' Chris said.

John is devoid of such drive, a man who, rather than building on his natural talent, squandered it to spend four years in the wilderness of the rankings. He was a fine weather player, who on his best days could play dream tennis.

Chris battles even when defeat stares her in the face, such as her extraordinary display in her debut in the 1971 US Open as an unknown sixteen-year-old against Mary Ann Eisel who was ranked no. 4 in the United States. Chris was 4–6, 5–6, 0–40 down; she saved six match points, hung on and clawed her way back to a 4–6, 7–6, 6–1 victory in front of a spellbound crowd of 10,000.

Nine years later she enthralled the Albert Hall during a Wightman Cup match; Virginia Wade was leading 7–5, 3–6, 5–1, 40–15, when Chris turned the tables and won the third set 7–5 and the match.

Defeat has a very different effect on both of them. John groans dejectedly that he ought to quit the game and Chris has had to talk him out of it on numerous occasions. If she loses, it strengthens her resolve never to let it happen again. 'John sees everyone playing much, much better than he is,' she said, 'and he gets it into his head that he is useless. In contrast, my attitude is that although I am no. 2 there's no reason why I can't be no. 1 again.'

Even when Martina Navratilova ousted her as the world's best and started to beat her in every match, Chris did not settle for being no. 2 or concede that her time as no. 1 was up. Nor did she plan to retire. Instead she changed her game, putting it on the offensive and coming into the net when beyond the service line was out of bounds to a baseliner. She incorporated new weapons into her game, expanded her selection of shots and made herself hungrier to win. She took up weightlifting and became fitter than she'd ever been and played better than she ever had until she inflicted a 6–2, 6–4 defeat on Martina in Florida in January 1985 – her first victory over her in two years.

Chris is a workaholic, a real pro in whatever she does, whether it's tennis, acting as President of the Women's Tennis Association, filming commercials for the companies whose products she endorses or TV commentating. In contrast, John has a predilection for unlimited relaxing in the sun or in front of the TV or video which she once feared could become a full-time occupation: 'He did it for a year and showed no signs of giving up.'

By mutual agreement John leaves most of the decision-making to Chris. 'Yes, love, whatever you want,' he replies when there is a decision to be made, and she appreciates his lack of possessiveness just so far. But, almost inevitably, when they had been married for a couple of years there came a time when she wished he'd be a bit more macho and fight for her.

Their tastes in movies and videos are as different as their tennis tactics. Miss Cool Chris loves nothing more than a little weep in front of a romantic or sentimental movie such as *Gone With The Wind*, while her tame 'Mr Nice Guy' husband could sit for hours relishing every detail of horror, sex and violence on video nasties like *I Spit On Your Grave*.

She married him for his qualities of kindness and thoughtfulness, and because he seemed so at peace with himself, which was such a relief after some of her previous lovers. She wanted a support partner, which was one of the reasons she hadn't married Jimmy Connors with his fixed ideas about the role of a wife. It would have meant Chris doing the tennis support part for him rather than the other way round.

When they got married John was an engaging but naïve twenty-four-year-old from Southend, who faced the triple problem of being the lesser-known husband of a famous wife, the poorer spouse of a multi-millionairess and a lesser player in the game she dominated.

But then there were also the conflicts and vulnerabilities Chris had to resolve within herself: the pull of her close family ties, the moral values and standards she'd been imbued with during a staunch Catholic upbringing. She had to reconcile these with the temptations and decadence of the international tennis circuit. The public had a 'Snow White' image of her, which didn't rest comfortably on her shoulders but which she had to live up to.

Chris revered and respected her father, who manages her money. She is inhibited from spending it on herself, yet extraordinarily generous about spending it on family and friends. When, at the age of twenty-eight and worth an estimated $10 million, Chris wanted to buy her first car, a Porsche, she got John to make the call to break the news to her father because she could imagine what he was going to say. 'I got him on the phone,' John said, 'and I couldn't get him off the subject of tennis. I couldn't get the words out; I was trying to find a way, and finally after about ten minutes of conversation he said, "It's good to hear from you, John," and I said, "Oh, by the way, Mr Evert, Chris has sort of seen this car out here and she really likes it and would like to buy it." There was a silence on the phone – I think he was hoping it was a Volkswagen or something. He said, "Well, that's fine; what sort of a car is it?" "Well actually it's a Porsche." "Ah well, she's never had a car before. Is it quite an expensive one?" I said, "It costs $45,000," and he said "Ah well, OK." Afterwards Chris felt so guilty about it, and I was amazed because she could have afforded four or five of them.'

Chris says her innate sense of economy is a hangover from her Catholic childhood, which taught her that materialism and temptations are evil. This is not the only characteristic of hers which seems incongruous in the context of the liberated circles of professional sport. She also has rather proper and slightly old-fashioned views about the conduct becoming to a wife. The thought that John might be upset made her decline a $100 bet from two of the younger 'boy crazy' girl tennis players to raid the men's locker room on a rainy afternoon at the Australian Open in 1984. She only reluctantly joined the girls when they made a massed invasion. Chris was relieved to find nobody undressed. 'I was afraid of someone saying to John, "Your wife walked in on us and we didn't have any clothes on." That's why I didn't want to do it.'

Chris has a quick wit and rarely misses an opportunity for a spot of humour, frequently coming out with *double entendres* or incisive one-liners. After dinner one evening during the 1984 US Open when they'd dropped into Rizzoli's, a late night Italian newsagents', for John to pick up the British papers he turned to her and asked,

'Have you read that book I gave you?' She retorted like lightning: 'How do you think I could have read a book when I've been watching your matches all week?' The quip was loaded with pride at John's defeat of two seeds and the fact that he had reached the quarter-finals – further than any Englishman in the US Open since Mark Cox in 1966.

As it happened, his demise at Flushing Meadow came as expected in the quarter-finals at the hands of Jimmy Connors, the defending champion who had won the US Open five times. He was almost certainly outside John's beatable range, even given the way he'd played throughout the Open, and John lost 7–5, 6–2, 6–0.

Once he was out of the tournament John switched to being a support partner to Chris to repay her loyal services. She'd beaten Carling Bassett in the semi-finals to face Martina Navratilova in the final. The world champion had already beaten her twelve consecutive times – a massive psychological hurdle to overcome, however much confidence Chris had in her game. As she prefers before a Grand Slam final, Chris relaxed in their hotel suite after dinner but the next day's final didn't dominate the evening.

'We don't normally talk much about the match the night before because Chris likes to psych herself up for the next day; she doesn't like to get her energy up too soon because then she gets tired, doesn't relax and doesn't sleep,' John explained. Players conserve their energy as a precious commodity before a big match. Jimmy Connors, for instance, doesn't even like to watch a movie the night before in case it stimulates his adrenalin too early and jeopardizes his performance on court, and Borg used to read comic books.

As they left the St Moritz Hotel to go to Flushing Meadow for the final, driven as they have been for some years by Don Barberi, John was in attendance in his usual 'helpmate' role but this time, for once, he could walk tall, proud of his own performance in the tournament in which his wife was a finalist.

'Although I subsequently lost to Martina the whole week had been a great start to getting back together again,' said Chris. 'I wouldn't have minded losing in the first round to have John do that well, because I've had a lot of success in my life and it was a great breakthrough for him.'

But life for them both – particularly in their marriage – had not always had this golden glow.

CHAPTER TWO

Beginnings

Chris Evert and John Lloyd were born within four months of each other in 1954 – she on 21 December and he on 27 August – 4,500 miles apart, Chris in Fort Lauderdale a mile from one of the best beaches in Southern Florida and John in Leigh-on-Sea, near Southend, Essex, on England's east coast overlooking the grey North Sea.

On paper their backgrounds were strikingly similar. Both came from large tennis-playing families – four of the Evert children won national junior championships and featured simultaneously in the American rankings, and the three Lloyd sons all played Davis Cup tennis for Britain.

Chris and John were both brought up in close-knit families and as adults have remained exceptionally family orientated. These common factors attracted them to one another when they first met because they automatically felt comfortable with someone from so familiar an environment, who had the same values.

Why Chris and John grew up to be respectively the iron lady, supreme victor of the court and the Mr Nice Guy who at times demonstrated how much talent and potential he had but at others lapsed into bouts of compulsively losing, is not only a result of their different genes, but also a reflection of their different parental influences, the contrast in discipline and competitive philosophies in the two households. It also indicates why more tennis champions are produced on the American side of the Atlantic than on the British.

During childhood Chris was conditioned to work at her tennis and to be a winner in the American super-competitive climate where victory is everything; John was brought up in a more relaxed fashion to compete at an amateur level where the British emphasis was on playing the game rather than going all out to win.

'When I was a child, I had three pairs of shoes – school shoes, Sunday shoes and tennis shoes,' Chris said, remembering that her early years in a strict, lower-middle class family had tended to be all work and no play. She had a controlled, industrious, sheltered upbringing: as the eldest daughter and second child in a family of five, life revolved around school, mass, tennis practice and the home. She went to mass every Sunday and grace is still said before meals.

Her mother, Colette, described the family's lifestyle: 'We were comfortable but we weren't wealthy. We ate plain food – I knew a lot of ways to cook chicken and hamburgers. We led a simple life but I never felt deprived and I don't think the children did either.'

Chris's father, Jimmy Evert, was the teaching pro at a municipal-owned complex of tennis courts in Holiday Park, five blocks from their home. It was his first job and the one he still has. He was responsible for starting Chris in tennis and gave her her first lessons in the school summer holidays when she was five and a half. He loved tennis and the people who played it, and had been immersed in the game from an early age.

He was third in a family of four boys, whose father was in the florists' business in Chicago, Illinois. Jimmy spent his formative years during the Depression when leisure and luxuries were rationed. 'I was a poor kid; my people didn't have much money,' he said, but young Jimmy was a self-starter.

Becoming a member of the nearby swish Chicago Town and Tennis Club was way beyond the family's means and the kids used to improvise at tennis by stringing up a net in the street behind their house. But Jimmy persisted and found a way of getting on to the real courts. 'I was the lucky kid in the neighbourhood who became the ballboy for the club. I was allowed to go and work there, chasing balls for six or seven hours a day, then I could use the courts and play on them.' The pro at the club, George O'Connell, helped Jimmy with his game and through him Jimmy was also able to play throughout the freezing northern winter, on indoor courts at a club on the other side of town. That entailed a daily tram ride of an hour and fifteen minutes each way but Jimmy didn't complain; he was thrilled to have the chance, and utilized it.

He became a skilled young player and won the National eighteen-and-under Indoor Championships; reached the last sixteen of the 1942 National Championships; and won the Canadian Singles Championship.

Tennis was a golden opportunity for Jimmy in an austere childhood. It was a challenge, it was a hobby and it offered the chance of travel, meeting people and playing in tournaments, all of which were treats beyond his reach otherwise. 'I really had some fun doing what I was doing, and I wanted my kids to have the same fun,' he said. 'I thought that tennis was a good way for them to occupy themselves. If they were going to get involved in athletics in any way this was the sport I wanted them to play. I didn't know if any of them would grow up to be a great player but that wasn't the point.'

Chris wasn't at all keen when her father announced to her that she was starting tennis lessons, because it meant the end of swimming and pool-side barbecues at the home of a young friend, Kara Bennett. 'I was hurt and crushed that my father took me away from my fun to throw tennis balls at me,' she remembered.

But sacrificing her hours of playtime jumping in the pool made Chris register that tennis entailed practice and a commitment. 'Dad would be right at the net, take balls out of a shopping basket and throw them gently at me. At first I didn't hit enough balls back to actually hit with other kids, but once I could it was more fun. Most of the time my Dad watched so I wanted to be good for him.'

From the day she walked on court she impressed her father

that when she got her racket on the ball she usually managed to get the ball back.

He instilled concentration and timing in her: 'I heard the same four phrases – "racket back, turn sideways, watch the ball, follow through" – over and over again for two years,' she said.

'I thought that probably Chris would grow up to be a pretty good junior player but that's as far as it went, no more than that,' Mr Evert remembered. 'She was quick both with her hands and feet, and she had a good head on her shoulders.'

Chris attended St Anthony's Junior School (where her mother helped serve the meals in the school canteen) until she was fourteen and then went on to St Thomas Aquinas High School in Fort Lauderdale which was run by Dominican nuns. Hours were from 8.30 am to 2.30 pm and then it was down to the courts for a couple of hours' practice, home, homework, supper and bed.

Ana Leaird, a contemporary of Chris's who has remained a close friend, remembered that she was a very good pupil. 'She was very smart, and was in a lot of advanced classes. The only one she didn't do too well in was home economics, which included sewing and cooking, because she was always struggling with hems and things. She somehow always finished the projects – Chrissie's not one to leave something unfinished – but I wouldn't say she excelled in it.'

By 1961 the Evert family had increased to four children – Drew, Chris, Jeanne and John (Clare was born in 1967). They soon needed a larger house and moved to a low ranch-style home at 1628 NE 7th Place where they lived until 1985 when they built a house on Florida's intra-coastal waterways less than two miles away.

It was a family home with a spacious L-shaped room with tennis rackets piled on a bench inside the front door, a formal sitting area, TV end and dining section; a bright, airy kitchen and large games room at the rear with glass doors into the small sunny garden. This latter room was dominated by a very striking giant-sized Andy Warhol pastel of Chris when she was twenty-three, one of a series of sports personalities including Mohammed Ali, Jack Nicklaus and Pele that Warhol had done.

Mr and Mrs Evert – who was the youngest of ten children and came from New Rochelle in New York – made the family the pivot of their lives and believed that a disciplined upbringing was the best start they could give their sons and daughters. Idleness wasn't tolerated and Mr Evert set an example: 'I always thought that the working day was from eight o'clock in the morning to eight o'clock at night, seven days a week. I think I was probably a strict parent. My mother always was with us and my dad too, and I felt a parent had to be that way. I realize that our children didn't have the freedom other children had.'

Another leisure activity which he curtailed, to Chris's disappointment, was staying overnight at friends' houses, because he knew that the kids stayed up late, talked into the night and woke up early, which meant they were too tired to be much good on the practice courts the following day.

'I explained to Chris that she couldn't do everything, and if she wanted to do all the fun things like go to tournaments she couldn't go out with her friends.'

He impressed on the children that as he was working overtime at the courts to pay tournament expenses and he and Mrs Evert were putting time and energy into their tennis education, they must also make sacrifices. This policy meant that Chris was allowed to go to fewer 'slumber parties' than some of her friends and had less of a sociable time because tennis, practice and tournaments were priorities.

Afternoons on the beach were rationed, too. Asked how often she went to the fabulous palm-fringed Atlantic beach a mile from their home, she said, 'Almost never; we were always playing tennis. Going to the beach was a real treat, something we did maybe twice a year.' It wasn't the permanent holiday lifestyle one might imagine in the recreational haven of Southern Florida, regarded as one of the world's playgrounds.

Chris found it hard to come to terms with the fact that her father was a tennis pro. 'All my girlfriends' fathers were doctors or lawyers or plumbers and I couldn't connect that my father was going out and playing tennis as his job.'

Chris actually changed his line of work for him when, aged six, she appeared on a local TV programme called *Skipper Chuck*. 'The presenter used to pick out one of the kids and ask them a few questions. He asked me, "What does your father do?" I was a little embarrassed so I said "He's a painter," but I meant an artist. When I got home my parents were laughing and asked why I had said that. I think it was a mixture of not wanting to say that he earned a living teaching tennis, and finding it hard to pronounce "tennis professional".'

Chris shared a sunny, cheerful bedroom with her sister Jeanne and they were reprimanded when it habitually became untidy – one of Chris's faults which she is still struggling to combat.

On court she had few weaknesses. Her father instilled in her the philosophy which formed the basis of her game – the player who makes the least errors usually wins – and the fundamental match tactic that on no account should you reveal your feelings to your opponent.

Chris competed in her first tournament the week of her eighth birthday at the annual Orange Bowl, staged at Flamingo Park, Miami Beach, the world's premier junior event, where she won the doubles with partner Bonnie Smith. There was close competition in the junior rounds in Florida in the early days of the tennis boom at the start of the sixties, and Chris soon got used to toughing out cliff-hanger matches.

Mrs Evert found her children's matches desperately nerve-racking, even more so than Chris's historic wins later on. 'You knew how much it meant to them, and you could see their eager little faces. Then they would think you were going to be disappointed and their eyes would fill up. When they're adult they can handle the strain, although I still get tense and feel for them, but the most crucial time for a tennis parent is when the children are starting out in junior tournaments. That's when they need support.'

Chris won the national fourteen-and-under singles in 1968 and thought there was already something automatic about her tennis playing. 'I felt, "wind me up and I'll walk on court",' she said.

John commented: 'She was programmed to be a champion,' while his initiation into the game was more happy-go-lucky. Chris attributes her early victories to simple hard graft. 'I practised so much that I was very accurate. I outsteadied everybody, and always hit one more ball back. Most of my success has been because I worked at my game.'

One of Chris's novelties was her two-handed backhand. Its origin was mainly logistical: she was too small and not strong enough to hold the racket with one hand. The courts at Holiday Park were clay, a surface which suited her and she suited it; she wasn't aggressive and she wasn't a particularly powerful player until she was a teenager. 'She could always hit a reasonably hard ball and get good pace on the ball, but she didn't have an over-powering game,' her father remembered.

It was because Chris was never outstandingly better than her rivals that her parents didn't consider her as world champion material. 'Even when she started having these phenomenal wins my husband and I still didn't think she was outstanding because the matches were so close. She was never on another plateau. She was always relaxed, and there was never any pressure on her – that's why her success happened,' Mrs Evert said.

As she grew older, Chris developed her own single-mindedness towards tennis, but as a teenager youthful curiosity tempted her to diversify into other activities and it was her father who stepped in to make her channel everything into her tennis.

'When I was about fourteen I wanted desperately to be a cheer-leader; I went to the try-outs and I was a sure bet to get in so I said to my parents, "I really want to try for it." My dad asked how much time it would entail – it was three afternoons a week for two or three months. He said, "All right, I think you have to make a choice: if you want to win matches and be a champion you're going to have to give that idea up and devote yourself to tennis, but if you want to do a lot of other things instead then it's up to you." I thought about it overnight – he was saying if you do cheer-leading I won't spend a lot of time with you on the courts.'

Her father only dimly recalled the incident: 'Chris didn't kick up a fuss. If she had and we'd given way maybe everything would have worked out the same, but maybe it wouldn't. I thought it was the best decision I could make for her at the time.'

Chris stuck to tennis, paying the price for getting to the top.

In retrospect she commented, 'I think what I missed out on was spending time with other kids away from tennis.'

Chris's breakthrough, which astonished her parents and the tennis world, came in North Carolina when she was fifteen and beat Margaret Court, thirteen years her senior and the no. 1 in the world. Only weeks before, Margaret had won the US Open which gave her the coveted Grand Slam, making her only the second woman after Maureen Connolly in 1953 ever to have achieved the feat of winning the four Grand Slam events in one year.

The promoter of the tournament in Charlotte, North Carolina had seen Chris and Laurie Fleming (another young junior and close friend of Chris's) play and had invited them there, basically to get some tournament experience.

'She only went with one change of clothes; we thought she'd be back the next day,' Mrs Evert recalled.

Laurie played first and, watched by Chris, acquitted herself impressively. 'She played Virginia Wade and lost 7–5, 6–3; everyone was saying, "Gosh, that's a good score." Then I played Françoise Durr and beat her 6–1, 6–0 and everybody was shocked,' Chris said, remembering that heady weekend. Durr was ranked no. 2 in the world on clay and was the outstanding, if unorthodox, French woman player of the sixties and seventies.

The following day in the semi-finals Chris played Margaret Court, the formidable Australian, a powerful athlete who had won Wimbledon in 1963, 1965 and 1970. Miraculously Chris wasn't paralysed with fright.

'I always felt sick in my stomach when I had to play girls my own age, but when I played someone ten years' older I thought that if I didn't win I still had ten more years, and that made me feel better. I get more nervous now when I think back to those days; it was unbelievable – I just never got nervous.

'I had nerves of steel that day, and I beat her 7–6, 7–6. It was a hell of a match; my groundstrokes and passing shots were great. I couldn't wait to phone my folks to tell them I'd beaten Margaret Court, no. 1 in the world. I dashed off the court and telephoned from the clubhouse. Dad was thrilled and said, "Let me get up off the floor!" Afterwards I was interviewed on TV and I thought, "I quite like this." I felt all the hours of work I'd put into tennis were worth it. I enjoyed the feeling of winning.'

'I was aghast,' her father remembered. 'In those days it was pretty unusual for a teenage player to do something amazing. We were all stunned by it, that she was starting to play so well against these top players. I also knew that it was only on clay, and I felt she might not be a very good grass player – especially with her two-handed backhand, which most people thought would not be a good stroke on grass.

'As it turned out, she wasn't all that bad and she handled herself better on that surface than on some others.'

Chris in fact has won five of her sixteen Grand Slam titles on grass – Wimbledons in 1974, 1976 and 1981 and the Australian Open in 1982 and 1984.

Mr and Mrs Evert flew up to Charlotte to watch Chris in the finals the following day in which she played Nancy Richey, one of the more colourful players on the circuit in those days. She was an outgoing Texan, famous for her shorts and peaked cap and a formidable clay-court player.

Chris lost the match 6–4, 6–1.

'The win had taken the wind out of her sails a little bit because she didn't play a good match; it wasn't bad but it wasn't as good as she had played against the other girls in the earlier rounds,' her father said.

It was an extraordinary experience for a fifteen-year-old – in twenty-four hours she'd had the triumph of a big win and the numbing disappointment of a finals defeat. Nancy Richey was a baseliner like Chris but an older and more experienced one, and her powerful groundstrokes absolutely exhausted the newcomer. Nancy was the first of only three players in Chris's entire career who have built up runs of consecutive victories over her. Tracy Austin was the second in 1979–80 and Martina Navratilova the third in 1982–5.

Chris regarded the first two as the more difficult opponents, even though their series of victories were considerably shorter than Martina's thirteen, because the only way she could beat them at the same baseliner game was to overpower them. Chris suffered five defeats at the hands of Nancy Richey before she pulled off her first win against her in the semi-finals of the US Clay Court Championships in the summer of 1975. Chris rallied from being 7–6, 5–0, 40–15 to take the second set 7–5 and be 4–2 up in the third before Nancy retired.

After Chris's victory over Margaret Court it was only a matter of time before she moved into the big league and that happened the following year, the summer of 1971, when her father said he saw her at her most ambitious. In the space of a few weeks she distinguished herself playing Wightman Cup, captured the eighteen-and-under National Championships and made her debut in the US Open.

She was the youngest player ever to be invited to play Wightman Cup. The annual women's match between the United States and Great Britain for an elegant silver trophy is named after its donor, Hazel Hotchkiss Wightman, who was one of the most successful American players during the years before and after the First World War. The competition was inaugurated in 1923 when Britain's Wimbledon champion, Kitty Godfree, played the legendary Helen Wills in a competition to mark the opening of the Stadium Court at the West Side Tennis Club, Forest Hills, New York. It is now played alternate years in Great Britain and the United States.

In Cleveland that year Chris whipped Virginia Wade, the British no. 1, 6–1, 6–1 in thirty-eight minutes and defeated Scottish Winnie Shaw 6–0, 6–4 in her singles rubbers to help the United States to a momentous 4–3 Wightman Cup victory.

Mrs Evert accompanied Chris while her father stayed at home in Fort Lauderdale baby-sitting for Chris's four brothers and sisters. He took the news of his daughter's brilliant performance in his stride and said at the time: 'The score was a little more decisive than I'd expected but Miss Wade is either hot or cold and today Chris had what it takes.'

The *Fort Lauderdale News* reported, 'Cool Chris freezes British', and the sixteen-year-old star admitted that she hadn't always been totally confident about the United States's chances of clinching the Cup. 'I didn't think we could do it. We just didn't have the big name players like they did.'

Little did Chris realize quite what a big name player she was soon to become.

John's early years were far less regimented and more relaxed than his future wife's. Home was a small semi-detached house a few minutes' walk up from the beach and Chalkwell station at Leigh-on-Sea, Essex, where he was the third of four children – elder sister Anne, brother David and younger brother Tony.

Neither of his parents had grown up locally; his father Dennis had lived at Galea Park some thirty miles away and his mother Doris came from a mining family in Durham. When they were both demobilized from the services after the war they decided to settle in Leigh-on-Sea, where they took on a flat, then when the children had been born the family moved to Woodfield Road, where Mr and Mrs Lloyd still live. Mr Lloyd, who had taken over his father's import/export business, commuted up to London daily.

'We didn't have a car so the house was convenient for the station, schools, the beach and the tennis club,' Mrs Lloyd said.

The family's social and recreational lives centred around the local tennis club at Westcliff-on-Sea, a simple but friendly establishment adjacent to the railway line. Mr Lloyd had taken up the game late in life and had reached Wimbledon qualifying standard before settling down to club level and coaching part-time at weekends. He had always been a keen sportsman. Cricket had been his game but he'd exchanged it for tennis after he'd got married because it meant he could spend more time with his family. Mrs Lloyd had learned to play because she realized that if she didn't she'd probably never see her husband.

'Tennis is the best family game of all,' Mr Lloyd maintains. 'When the children were growing up we'd go down to the club, I'd play one set and Mum would be on babysitting duty and then we'd swop.'

David Lloyd joked about his parents' Sunday matches against each other: 'You could guarantee that lunch would be in stony silence with the loser not speaking to the winner.'

John first picked up a racket at Westcliff-on-Sea Tennis Club when he was about six and started messing around on court. His brother David, six years his senior, already had a promising junior career going. Mrs Lloyd remembered that when John was only two or three and hitting stones with a stick on the pebbly Essex beach he'd rarely missed, and a friend of theirs had commented on his sense of timing.

John had it on court too: 'He used to hit the ball over the net automatically; he could play tennis from the beginning,' his mother said, and he became hooked on the game because it was something he could do well. All his drawings at Chalkwell Primary School contained something to do with tennis, and one teacher wrote in his exercise book, 'Wouldn't it be nice, John, to hear you say you want to do something other than play tennis!'

John's primary school headmaster pinpointed John's most engaging personal quality which has made him so popular all his life, foreseeing that it would be a flaw in his on-court career. 'John's wonderful but he's too nice ever to become a top tennis player,' he said.

Both parents had an input into their sons' game. Mr Lloyd used to coach them while Mrs Lloyd – the more competitive parent, having been brought up as one of twelve children – was the driving force behind the practice sessions. 'Mum got you out, then Dad did the technical side,' David remembered.

'I think I played every night with them up to junior Wimbledon standard,' Mrs Lloyd said. 'I didn't have the shots but I used to hit loads of balls to them, and when they got too good I just used to throw balls up in the air for them to smash.'

Two factors had a strong bearing on the way John was brought up: he was the third child and second son so, as in many families, received much more lenient treatment than his elder brother, David. In addition, John was docile whereas David was a highly-strung, temperamental boy which meant he needed a lot of reprimanding.

John learned early how to cash in on his blond good looks. 'He was easy; he smiled his way through life and you couldn't hit him. David could never understand why John never got thrashed,' Mr Lloyd said, but he admitted, 'John was always lazy. David used to say to him, "Come into the kitchen and help wash-up," and he'd actually take one dish and sit on a stool and dry it.'

John got away with doing pretty much as he pleased and cultivated his taste for television at an early age; he would lie on the sitting-room floor, gazing at the screen while devouring whole packets of breakfast cereal. 'We used to call him the Sugar Smack King,' his mother remembered.

John and David were entirely different both on and off court. 'John's talent was with the racket, whereas mine was that I hated to lose more than anything else so I kept going. If I'd had his skill and he'd had my temperament then we could have been very good players,' David said.

Mr Lloyd was tough on David and never gave in to him but was the reverse with John and seldom pushed him into anything. 'I didn't need to be told to train, to go on a run or to practise because I did them on my own; John did need to be told but he never was,' David remembered.

John acknowledged that perhaps he could have been a better player if he'd been pushed, but thought that it might have backfired and he'd have given up tennis altogether because his main motivation was that he enjoyed playing and it wasn't a chore.

Being David's younger brother ensured that he was given a hard time from his first day at Southend High School. David had been a rogue at school: 'I think I was probably summoned in to see the headmaster more than anyone else,' he remembered. The teachers made it clear that they wouldn't put up with any similar nonsense from Lloyd junior and he was caned during his first week as a warning.

John loathed school and lessons and after trying for a short while he regularly played truant a couple of days a week to go off to the cliff-tops or the movies. His elder sister, Anne, helped him forge the obligatory sick notes. He kept very quiet at school about even playing tennis, let alone being good at it, because it was considered a cissy sport. The fact that he was better at it than the senior boys did nothing to enhance his popularity with them.

John did well in junior tournaments because he was such a tennis natural. 'Unfortunately I got used to coasting because I was always near the top in my age group,' he said.

Whereas Chris learnt young what competitiveness and close matches were, John took a recreational attitude towards his game and was fairly slack about practice. He skipped it if it was raining, if he didn't feel like it or if he wanted to go and kick a ball around on the football pitch instead.

He also had far less opportunity than Chris to practise. She used to peer up into the cloudless Florida sky praying for rain so she could have a day off. John frequently couldn't even get on to the frost covered courts for months in winter.

A couple of weeks before his eleventh birthday John reached the final of the national under-fourteens championships at Exmouth. He lost to fellow Essex player Stephen Warboys, who was his main junior rival along with Buster Mottram, but they came in for some praise in the sports pages for the calibre of their match. 'It is unusual to find two boys, barely teenagers, producing lawn tennis skills to hold a crowd with Wimbledon-type excitement,' the *Daily Telegraph* said.

He was runner-up the following two years too, which prompted Dan Maskell to doubt whether he had winning potential. 'A lot of the sports writers thought that John was too nice to win the big one; they used to call him Mr Runner-Up,' Mrs Lloyd remembered.

John Barrett, who had been Britain's Davis Cup captain from 1959 to 1962 and had married Angela Mortimer, the 1961 Wimbledon champion, gave John an enormous amount of help and training as a teenager. He had coached a junior squad of boys, including David Lloyd, to create a well of talent from which to select future Davis Cup teams. They became known as the 'Barrett Boys' and although the group was disbanded before John's time, Barrett gave him similar tuition.

When he was thirteen John used to travel up on the train and tube from Southend to London every Friday where he was met by John and taken to the Barrett's Wimbledon flat. The following morning he was woken up early for a run on Wimbledon Common followed by a cold bath, which he never used to enjoy. After breakfast they made their way to the courts. The first time they played on a chilly winter's day one incident told John Barrett a lot about his new pupil.

'I'd got a large basket of balls so I said to him, "Go down that end – we'll loosen up and get the blood flowing." We started hitting and after five or ten minutes the basket was empty and the balls were spread all round the court. I started to pick them up at my end and roll them up towards the basket. I looked down the far end and saw that John was standing in the middle of the baseline with his legs crossed, leaning on his racket. I said, "Hey, what about picking the balls up your end?" He said, "Oh, I never ball-boy." I said, "Well listen, young man, if you're going to play with me at all any more you'll damn well pick the balls up." So rather sheepishly he went to collect them. I thought then that rather summed him up. It told me that he hadn't been trained to do these things and rather suggested he was spoiled, both as a player and I think in other ways.'

Barrett was impressed with the younger Lloyd's flair. 'His fore-hand was his big shot; he could hit it instinctively on the rise. His backhand was a very natural shot too, but it wasn't as penetrating as his forehand. He was a natural volleyer; he moved very well and leaped for smashes; he was light on his feet.'

John Barrett spotted John's potential even though he usually lost to Stephen Warboys who was regarded as the most promising junior of his era and whose father spent thousands of pounds trying to make him a Wimbledon champion. Barrett predicted that John would go further than Stephen and has been proved right. Warboys faded quickly as a senior player and John has gone on to have a much longer and more successful career.

John was fortunate in that he made many friends who genuinely wanted to help him since he was a likeable talented youngster. When money was tight David used to hitch his way round the tournament circuit, once thumbing lifts back through the night from Torquay to Leigh-on-Sea where he had to play the next morning, whereas John always managed to be taken. This routine toughened up an already fighting David but did little to instil in John the steel and drive he didn't have.

The parents of Ashley Compton-Dando (who was a close friend of John's and a fellow junior player) were especially good to John. Mrs Lloyd remembers touring with her youngest son Tony, economizing in bed and breakfast accommodation while John was with the Compton-Dandos in a five-star hotel.

John was determined to extricate himself from school – which he saw as rather superfluous to his needs – at the earliest possible time. He did so at the age of fifteen and a half without achieving academic distinction. His absenteeism and distaste for lessons in practically every subject told in his mock O-levels. In the first two maths exams he handed in blank papers which resulted in a threat from the headmaster that if he did the same in algebra he would be caned. So John wrote screeds and screeds of unmathematical rubbish and even astonished his friends by going up and requesting more paper. As a result he escaped a caning but his marks were still nought out of a hundred.

Out of school, John was able to concentrate on his tennis, but it would be some years before his name featured prominently on the sports pages, unlike that of Chris Evert. Over four thousand miles away the sixteen-year-old from Fort Lauderdale was about to become an overnight sensation and monopolize the sporting headlines.

If ever there was a stage ready for the arrival of a new star it was the US Open at the West Side Tennis Club in Forest Hills in 1971. This tournament was to become a turning point in Chris's career and a landmark in the history of tennis.

The top three tennis players – Margaret Court, Billie Jean King and Rosie Casals – had all dominated the game for some years and were in their mid- to late-twenties. Margaret Court had pulled out because she was pregnant and the new youthful star, Evonne Goolagong, who had won Wimbledon weeks before, wasn't coming. The absence of Rod Laver and Ken Rosewall deprived the men's draw of star names.

Chris, a fresh-faced teenager, was far from welcome in the locker room in the Tudor-style clubhouse. She was feminine with her coloured hair ribbons which matched the trim on her pretty dresses, and neat gold earrings in her pierced ears. In contrast, the other women seemed butch feminists. She was a baseliner when serve and volleying were all the vogue. And she was an amateur and a threat to the pros in the year the women, led by Billie Jean King, had taken on the tennis establishment to fight for a better financial deal and equality with the men players.

In 1970, two years after open tennis had come in, the women's game was in the shadow of the men's, and their prize money was still way behind. The Pacific South West Championship was the catalyst for action when that year it offered a $7,500 purse for women and $60,000 for men. Billie Jean King and Rosie Casals approached Gladys Heldman, then editor and publisher of *World Tennis* magazine, who set up an alternative women's championship in Houston. The United States Tennis Association suspended the participants. 'Women's Lob', they were called, and a new circuit had arrived. The problem this posed for Chris, who under USTA rules couldn't turn pro until her eighteenth birthday, was that if she played the Women's Lob circuit she would be suspended from USTA-sanctioned events including Wimbledon and the US Open, and as an amateur she couldn't accept any prize money so was depriving the other players.

When she shot to fame in the 1971 Open the resentment only increased. In the second round Chris faced Mary Ann Eisel, ranked no. 4 in the United States, and as her opponent served at 6–4, 6–5, 40–0 Chris wondered about the correct way for a loser to walk off court: 'Should I smile at the ten-thousand crowd or look dignified and serious?'

However, Chris fended off six match points to level at 6-all in the second set which meant a tie-breaker. She won this followed by the third set, 6–1. It was a stupendous performance and made her the darling of the crowds but when she returned to the locker room she was ostracized. Hardly any of the other players spoke to her. Even Ingrid Bentzer, who did, remembers her sitting with her shoulders hunched as if she were cold, isolated by the black looks and frosty vibes which travelled in her direction. The only way that Chris knew how to deal with such treatment was to grin and bear it.

Chris was credited with bringing in the record gate at the tournament. People converged on the stadium court for her matches and dispersed afterwards, and the crowd was unanimously pro Chris which infuriated her opponents.

In the third round she beat Françoise Durr, 2–6, 6–2, 6–3. 'You think this is fair?' Frankie complained in her strong French accent in the locker room after the match, livid that the pro-Chris crowd had cheered her double faults.

Chris beat Lesley Hunt in the quarter-finals to face Billie Jean King in the semis. Chris's opponent, an advocate of a better deal for women pros, couldn't afford to be beaten by a sixteen-year-old amateur and at 4.30 pm on 10 September, 1971 Chris's charmed run in the 1971 US Open came to an end when she shook hands with Billie Jean at the net after her 6–3, 6–2 victory. Billie Jean had played brilliantly, with some very cunning tactics which Chris had no answer to. 'She kept slicing the ball and doing all sorts of smart little shots which frustrated me because I wasn't used to that,' Chris remembered.

During that momentous week the American media had foisted a list of nicknames on Chris including 'Cinderella in Sneakers' and 'Miss Apple Pie'. Chris was regarded as the girl next door, Sugar'n' spice and everything nice. She handled herself with an extraordinary aplomb, far beyond her sixteen years, but she didn't especially enjoy those early press conferences. 'I just remember going in and seeing a hundred people who were all shoving microphones in my face. My answers were usually really simple, a few words like, "She played well," because I hadn't had much experience answering questions. When I saw those big men with cigars I didn't want to reveal myself; I just wanted to answer the questions and get out.'

Ted Tinling was one person who was tremendously impressed by her cool in press conferences. 'She demolished the impressive television commentators who, in those days, were much grander than the players they were talking to. Chrissie used to put them down with clever one-liners. After she'd defeated Lesley Hunt in the quarter-finals one of them said, "Miss Evert, we noticed that when you changed ends you didn't sit down. Does that mean you think you're much fitter than everybody else?" She gave him a cold look and said, "No, there wasn't anything to sit on."' In the press conference after her final defeat in the US Open she said, 'I'm sorry it's all over but I have to go back to school now.'

Chris showed an early respect for grass, the surface on which she later won five Grand Slam titles.

John playing at the Junior All England Championships at Wimbledon in 1968. *Associated Newspapers Ltd*

Love doubles: (above) Chris and fiancé Jimmy Connors both win Wimbledon in 1974. *Michael Cole Camerawork*

(Below) Chris and her husband John having just beaten Bjorn Borg and Mariana Simionescu. *Newspix International*

(Opposite) Bride and bridegroom in April 1979.

John and Chris
in action
(above) *Tommy
Hindley*; (below)
*Michael Cole
Camerawork*

Back in Fort Lauderdale she was fêted. Journalists, photographers and television crews trailed her from class to class at school and the media spotlight was turned on the Evert family. Chris said she managed to keep her feet firmly on the ground throughout the adulation because of the way her parents handled it and the security of her upbringing.

'I was safe in the cocoon of my parents' home and under their influence. I didn't want to go to school the day after we got back from New York but they firmly insisted. I still made my bed and cleaned my room and folded the socks. I didn't think big of myself.'

Mr Evert, who was polite, co-operative and accommodating to the journalistic hordes who turned up on the doorstep, knew when enough was enough and took the phone off the hook. 'As much as we appreciate all the attention given our household there comes a time when you must shut out the world and catch up on being a family,' he explained. He made it clear that normal life must go on: 'I don't want to be rude but I've got to get some rest at night. I've got five kids. They've got homework to do.'

Mr and Mrs Evert's determination to preserve normality at home and not to let the adulation mesmerize them didn't mean that they weren't extraordinarily proud of her. 'We marvelled at everything she did at the Open. As a father I would have been happy if she had won the national under-eighteens',' said Mr Evert.

Chris had her own sense of priorities which kept her success in perspective: 'The big compliment wasn't being written about in *Sports Illustrated*; it was being praised by my peers. The congratulations of the kids in school made me feel one of them, which I hadn't before because I'd been away at tournaments so much. It's very important for a teenager to be accepted by her peers.'

Her mother remembers that winning 'the most likely to succeed' and 'the most popular' awards at school meant more than anything else to her. They still stand on the shelves in Chris's bedroom surrounded by framed rackets with which she has won Wimbledon, a miniature replica of the Wimbledon's Women's Singles plate and many other of the world's most prestigious awards.

Many miles away, John read of Chris's acclaim as the new tennis heroine, little dreaming that one day she would be his wife. He was living in the YMCA in Wimbledon and struggling round the Torquay, Exmouth, Bournemouth provincial round of tournaments far below the big-time Grand Slam events.

CHAPTER THREE

On the Way Up

'I took my homework to tournaments until I was eighteen,' Chris said, and she acknowledges that having to remain in school and not being able to turn pro until her eighteenth birthday have contributed to the marathon length of her career.

1985 will be her fourteenth Wimbledon, in contrast to some of the youngsters of the eighties who followed her example as a teenage prodigy and who have only managed sprint-length spells in top tennis. 'From the age of fifteen to eighteen I played about five women's tournaments a year; I paced myself and didn't burn myself out. Today some of the younger players have turned pro by the time they're fifteen which means playing full-time on the circuit for thirty weeks of the year. Mentally that's tough because as children they're thrown in with twenty-five- and thirty-year-old women. And physically it's bad because they're not fully developed so one injury becomes a recurring one and stays with them for the rest of their lives.' Tracy Austin is one player who, in 1979 aged sixteen, became the youngest player ever to win the US Open and made a million dollars before her seventeenth birthday. Injury and being 'burned out' have since chequered her career.

Chris attributes her injury-free career to good luck and having taken care of herself. 'I have a good frame for tennis. I'm built well, I have good balance and my style of play isn't to throw myself all over the court but is based on consistency and accuracy rather than acrobatics. I've also had the good sense to go to a physiotherapist and get treatment whenever I've had a twinge. And I've always taken precautions: I'm a firm believer in regular massages.'

Chris also derived a tremendous psychological advantage from her controlled and gradual entry into the game; she didn't take on the best players in the world until she was old enough to have a realistic chance of beating them.

'At the age of fourteen there's no way you're going to beat the current champion because she's going to be much stronger than you are, so if you play her you start your career with a losing record and the memory of that never really leaves you,' she said.

Chris never built up a losing record. It was a mere six months later – at their next meeting – that she avenged her defeat by Billie Jean King at the US Open semi-final by beating her in the final of the Tennis Club Women's International Tournament in Fort Lauderdale.

It was on clay – her surface – at Holiday Park, her father's club and in front of her own supporters. The spectator space was packed and people perched in the trees, sat on rooftops and climbed up into a half-built apartment complex next to the courts in order to see the match.

Australian Judy Dalton, who was a Wimbledon semi-finalist in 1968 and who lost to Chris in the semi-finals 6–1, 6–3 remembered Chris's standard of play: 'She was very clever; no matter how hard you concentrated she was always there and if you let your concentration lapse you were gone. Her strategy was just to let people make mistakes. We all knew she'd always get the ball back.'

Chris didn't disappoint her fans, and she decimated Billie Jean 6–1, 6–0. 'Good luck to all you two-handed backhand kids,' she said afterwards, which was also a reference to Chris's younger sister, Jeanne who had beaten Rosie Casals in the first round of the same tournament.

The following month, in March, Chris played in a tournament at the T-Bar-M Racket Club in Dallas, Texas and met the twenty-one-year-old Wimbledon champion, Evonne Goolagong for the first time. Tennis scribes had described them as dissimilar as night and day – one the cool mechanical American, the other the smiling instinctive player from the dusty Australian outback.

Chris was very inquisitive about the player who (she had heard) used to have a newspaper clipping of her idol Margaret Court – whom Evonne had beaten to win her first Wimbledon crown in 1971 – pinned to the bush-shack she shared with seven aboriginal brothers and sisters. 'Her story was like a fairytale. I thought about her a lot, and I even wanted to write to her. She said in an article that she was curious to meet me, too. I remember my first impression of her. She was wearing this flimsy top without a bra and was really natural. She used to walk around carrying a transistor radio, her hair was all messy and she had a crooked tooth. She didn't seem to care what other people thought and I admired her for that,' Chris said.

Ted Tinling likened the projected Evert–Goolagong clash in the Dallas semi-final to the legendary meeting between Helen Wills and Suzanne Lenglen in Cannes in 1926, but there was one obstacle to be overcome before Chris played Evonne – Billie Jean King.

She defeated Chris 6–7, 6–3, 7–5 in the quarter-finals and was welcomed in the locker-room as if she had just won Wimbledon for having quashed the teenage newcomer whom the women players all still regarded as an unwelcome outsider.

Chris was crushed – defeat combined with their bitchiness was too much – and she went into the toilet to cry. Standing at a wash-basin splashing water on her tear-stained face she felt a comforting hand on her shoulder. It was Evonne. 'Don't worry, it's just a tennis match; don't be so upset,' she said kindly and Chris was touched.

But it was only a postponement of their meeting on court and the first Evert–Goolagong match took place four months later at Wimbledon. Chris, in contrast to Evonne – who had hummed along to the music on her radio during lunch before the match – was very nervous. 'I was amazed that she was singing yet I was a nervous wreck,' Chris said.

It was Chris's first Wimbledon and Evonne's third, and the

Centre Court seemed filled with adoring Goolagong fans who wouldn't warm to Chris with her icy exterior and ruthless killer instinct which were so un-British.

She was likened to Maureen Connolly, 'Little Mo', who was also a baseliner with an iron will to win and had succeeded young, winning the US Singles when she was sixteen and going on to win Wimbledon in 1952, 1953 and 1954.

Chris lost the semi-final match against Evonne 4–6, 6–3, 6–4, and afterwards she said, 'I never resented the fact that the crowds were for Evonne, but I was envious. I wanted to shout, 'Don't you know I'm feeling something inside too?'' I was tight-lipped and didn't crack a smile while Evonne laughed at the fact that she sometimes forgot the score.'

Chris's visit to England for Wimbledon 1972 and the Wightman Cup immediately before it was Chris's first, and she found the country untouched by the American tennis boom and the pace of life decidedly lackadaisical. 'All the tennis players in the States were wearing pastel-coloured clothes while in England they were still in their whites, some wearing long pants and all playing with little wooden rackets. England seemed to be behind the States by about ten or fifteen years. I thought people in general were very polite and courteous and very old-fashioned in the way they talked. I sensed right away that there was no competition in the air and it was going to be an easy life compared to America,' Chris said.

It was in this rather backward climate that Chris's future husband was slowly making his way up the tennis ladder via an apprenticeship of junior tournaments and under-twenty events such as the Galea Cup, an international team competition.

In March 1972 John was one of a squad of boy players who toured the Riviera tournaments in the South of France sponsored by a BP International Tennis Fellowship. But already other countries' young players had far overtaken their British counterparts in terms of training and competition exposure. John Barrett remembered that the Swedes were particularly advanced: 'Well before us Lennart Bergelin, Borg's coach, used to drive Borg and a bus-load of young Swedish players around. Borg was an absolute menace to them because he would never stop practising. They were always late everywhere because he would still be on the practice court and Lennart would have to go and drag him off. Neither the other Swedish boys nor ours practised with the same intensity. I think that's what John has always lacked, any real urgency or intensity; he's a very laid-back individual.

'He was modestly ambitious but I don't think he saw himself as the world's no. 1 so he wasn't prepared to make the effort and sacrifice that would have entailed. He likes the easy life; he doesn't like pushing himself.'

It wasn't that John couldn't pull out the stops when an occasion demanded it. John Feaver, who shared an Earlsfield flat with John and a group of other players for a while, remembers a Lawn Tennis Association junior training week at Lilleshall Hall in the Midlands.

There was a run each morning, which John detested. 'Lloyd would turn up in his mittens and lope along at the back and always be last,' John said. On the final day the LTA coach, Tony Mottram, announced that whoever was last would have to go round again. That put the run into an entirely different perspective as far as John was concerned. 'It was mittens off and he kicked into overdrive and streaked in first,' Feaver said.

John won his first prize money of £350 in October 1972 at the Dewar Cup at Billingham on Teesside. In the women's final Margaret Court beat Julie Heldman but it was John's victory over the stronger, more experienced Pat Cramer of South Africa which attracted all the attention. 'The men's final produced a result like something out of fiction,' Henry Raven wrote in the *Daily Telegraph*. 'In terms of match-playing ability he was astonishingly mature, shrewd and consistent for his years. Here was a performance to give the British men's game some genuine hope.'

'That was my breakthrough,' John remembered, and he used the prize money to go to the States to widen his experience.

Chris's disappointment at her loss to Evonne in the Wimbledon semi-finals was eased by the fact that she had fallen head over heels in love with Jimmy Connors, who she had really got to know for the first time during the tournament.

Three years older than Chris, 'Jimbo' was as outspoken and brash as Chris was shy and prim. During Chris's stay in London they danced in a hotel discothèque after the Wightman Cup dinner, had dinner in the Rib Room at the Carlton Tower Hotel and partied at the Playboy Club in Park Lane. There was plenty of common ground in their tennis careers, as Chris pointed out: 'His mother had taught him and my father had taught me; we'd both learnt on public courts. Jimmy was very highly tuned and intense about his tennis at a young age and so was I. We paralleled one another all the way up in the juniors.'

Chris had first met Jimmy when she was ten, playing in the Orange Bowl Junior Championships in Miami. Years before that, Mr Evert had taken out Jimmy's mother Gloria when they were both growing up in Chicago.

Chris's boyfriend before she'd left for London had been Bob Marley, a basketball player at the same high school. He learned about Chris's new romance when he opened his newspaper in Fort Lauderdale, and he telephoned Chris's close friend Ana Leaird to find out what was going on.

'All of a sudden Bob called me up because he'd read that she and Jimmy were in love. I phoned her in London – which in those days was quite something – and Chris told me that she had just met Jimmy and been out to dinner with him. It was definitely love at first sight; her stomach just went into butterflies when she saw him. He was all the things she wasn't and he represented everything she wished she could be. He was flamboyant and wore his heart on his sleeve. With Chris everything stopped for Jimmy. Bob definitely looked like an ex-boyfriend.'

Chris said: 'It was a crush; I think it must always be special and exciting with the first guy you fall in love with. I'm glad it happened with Jimmy because he was great; we had a wonderful time, and we were perfectly suited to each other for that period.'

Back in Fort Lauderdale Chris's life began to revolve around the absent Jimmy which amazed some of her friends because she'd always been so controlled about her emotions. Ana Leaird wasn't surprised: 'I think that side of her had always been there; Jimmy just brought it out. Her whole life used to come to a stop when he called. She scheduled her practice around the time he was most likely to ring. If he was half-an-hour late she'd panic, worried that he wasn't going to call her that day, then the phone would go and afterwards everything would revert to normal.'

The following year Chris travelled the international circuit chaperoned by her mother and Mrs Connors accompanied Jimmy. The presence of both mothers stifled Jimmy and Chris's affair and particularly frustrated Chris.

'My mom and I had a little falling out because my parents felt that I needed to be chaperoned at all times. When I was with Jimmy we were never allowed to be alone. I wasn't even allowed to go to his room to watch a TV programme, and I resented that.'

The romantic dinners *à deux* which Chris longed for became tedious foursomes with both mothers present and it strained mother-daughter relations to the limit. 'It got to the point where I wouldn't talk to my mother. I ignored her, and cut her out of the conversation.'

Even the strait-jacket of Chris's upbringing and a disciplined tennis player's tunnel vision couldn't prevent some adolescent reactions and emotions surfacing and they resulted in a spate of defeats in Europe in the summer of 1973.

Chris lost to Margaret Court in the French final, vented her moodiness by messing up her match against Evonne Goolagong in the Italian Open, and followed this by losses in England to Julie Heldman in a grass court tournament in Nottingham, Virginia Wade at Queen's Club and Billie Jean King 6–0, 7–5 in the final at Wimbledon.

Her mother remembered that the run of losses taught her something about life too. 'During that period she wondered where all her friends had disappeared to, so I reminded her that everyone loves a winner.'

By October, when Chris hadn't seen Jimmy since the US Open, she found the separation unbearable. 'I felt that I had to see him; I was lonely and my parents didn't understand what I was going through.' So Chris literally ran away from home. Ana Leaird gave her a lift to the airport where she caught a plane to Los Angeles to join Jimmy, leaving Ana to deliver a hastily scribbled note of explanation to her parents.

They were hurt and alarmed but allowed Chris to travel with Ana to South Africa later in the year where Chris and Jimmy were playing in the South African Open. Both won, and Jimmy proposed, spending part of his winnings on buying Chris an engagement ring at a diamond factory.

Jimmy and Chris's love-story rolled on for another seven months to Wimbledon in 1974 where Chris didn't think she had a chance of success because she hadn't beaten Billie Jean King or Evonne Goolagong on grass courts. Nevertheless she said to Jimmy over dinner – celebrating the second anniversary of their first date by having dinner again at the Rib Room at the Carlton Tower Hotel – 'Wouldn't it be great if we could both win Wimbledon?'

That weekend in the finals Chris beat Russian Olga Morozova 6–0, 6–4 and Jimmy beat Ken Rosewall 6–1, 6–1, 6–4.

At nineteen Chris was Wimbledon champion and no. 1 in the world. She had come to the tournament with a run of thirty straight singles victories, two of them the Italian and French Open titles. She was on a high – overwhelmingly in love yet still very single-minded about her tennis. 'It seemed quite natural for me to be no. 1 in the world because I'd always been no. 1 in the juniors. I thought that as long as I kept a level head and never looked back I could remain at that position but if I started thinking how great I was or celebrating a little too much I'd lose that vital momentum.'

Jimmy, at twenty-one, was also no. 1 in the world and his prowess inspired Frank Deford to write in *Sports Illustrated* magazine: 'Conqueror was what he was, because Connors did not merely win. He assaulted the opposition, laid waste to it, often mocked it as well, simply by the force of his presence. The other players feared to go against him, because the most awesome legend that can surround any player sprang up about Connors: the better any mortal played against him, the better Connors became.'

Even now Chris talks about her first Centre Court triumph with an air of disbelief. 'It was a thrill but I was only nineteen and I didn't realize the true significance of it. It was more of a romantic thing, the fairytale of Jimmy and I winning it together. It was the first time sweethearts had won Wimbledon at the same time. Sharing the win with someone I loved, rather than the individual victory, made it seem more important to me.'

But it was a highlight of Chris's father's life. He was in Fort Lauderdale so had to wait until the following day to watch the match on television, but he spoke to Chris on the telephone when she came off court. 'She called right after the match; it was a very touching moment. That was probably the most moving event in her whole career, something we had never dreamed could possibly happen.'

At the Wimbledon Ball the band played 'The Girl That I Marry', and Chris and Jimmy opened the dancing – Chris balancing precariously on trendy sandals with six-inch heels which she'd bought in the King's Road because she thought they made her look taller.

The wedding was set for 8 November that year but five weeks before in a fraught, six-hour phone call they agreed to postpone it. Although they were still in love a lot of 'buts' had crept in.

'Part of the problem was that Jimmy had certain ideas about the role of a wife and I didn't want to give up tennis completely and settle down and have children,' Chris said. Billie Jean King made Chris aware of another point of view. Despite the rivalry between them, Billie Jean was one of the first to see how good Chris was for women's tennis and how the publicity she received could benefit all the players and the game. She and Chris played doubles for a time and she remains a player whom Chris both admires and respects.

'I talked to her a couple of times about it, and she said, "You're very young; you've got your whole life ahead of you. If you want to play tennis and have a career don't get tied down."

'I think that Jimmy and I are alike; we are both ambitious and we have goals. Perhaps two people who are so intense would just kill each other in a marriage.'

Eleven years later she said, 'I don't think it would have worked; I really don't.'

Chris telephoned home with the news of the postponed wedding, which later became a broken engagement, the day before Mrs

Evert was going to post the wedding invitations. Both parents were relieved, and the invitations are still around and being used for scrap paper in the Evert house.

Mrs Evert described the decision as an answer to a prayer. 'My husband and I both thought they were too young but we couldn't say so because then they would have eloped and it probably would have ended up in a divorce. I admired them so much, because another couple might have gone ahead and got married. She and Jimmy had the guts to call it off.'

John had also had a broken engagement with another tennis player as a teenager. While touring Australia and New Zealand at the age of nineteen he had fallen in love with Swedish junior Isabel Larsson. She was half-Swedish and half-Spanish with dark hair, brown eyes and dressed in the current fashion of white boots and mini skirts. 'I think we got carried away by the romantic New Zealand islands,' John remembered. Certainly once John and Isabel were back in their respective Northern Hemisphere homes the impossibility of the engagement was clear to both of them and was broken amicably.

John's tennis career was progressing satisfactorily in an upward direction. In 1973 he featured in the Lawn Tennis Association's official British rankings for the first time – at no. 8. He had also made the major and very commendable jump from doing well in Britain to proving himself thoroughly competitive on the international circuit which even then was an infinitely tougher league.

That year he played in the French Open, Wimbledon and the US Open for the first time with encouraging success.

Wimbledon 1973 was ravaged by controversy because Yugoslav Nikki Pilic had been suspended by the International Lawn Tennis Federation after refusing to play for Yugoslavia in the Davis Cup. This prompted a boycott by thirty-five men players including eight of the singles seeds, which left rather a barren draw.

John was affected by all the politicking when pressure was put on him to withdraw, too – which he refused to do. Largely thanks to the boycott, John did as well that year as he's ever done and reached the third round. In the first he disposed of former French junior François Caujolle, followed by Australian Keith Hancock in the second before losing to Indian Vijay Amritraj in the third.

John's inaugural Wimbledon introduced him to the taxing demands a British player faces trying to live up to the expectations of his home crowd.

'A British player faces triple the pressure of any other player. It's *the* event, the only one which really matters. Sometimes you feel as though the whole year depends on that fortnight. The crowd expects me to do well and wants me to do well; if I hit a winner it's all applause, if I lose a point it's "aaaaahs" and groans. I come off with my head splitting.'

John started 1974 in fine form by wrecking the seeding pattern of the New South Wales' Men's Lawn Tennis Championship in Sydney by defeating the no. 2 seed, Australian John Alexander. It was one of two triumphs by British players: Mark Farrell had eliminated the no. 3 seed, Bjorn Borg.

John went on to win against former Wimbledon champion Frank Sedgman, who was more than twice his age, on his way to the semi-finals.

In May John was selected to play Davis Cup tennis for Britain for the first time, in a team which included his brother David, John Feaver and Mark Farrell. The match was against Egypt in Cairo. It was the first time since Laurie and Reggie Doherty before the First World War that brothers had played together in the Davis Cup team for Britain. The Dohertys are regarded as the founding fathers of the game and the Doherty Gates at the south-west entrance of the All England Club commemorate them.

Although Britain was routed 5–0 in Cairo that year, the experience impressed John that playing Davis Cup was something special. It's an international team competition which dates back to 1900, played for a mammoth silver punch bowl lined with gold, named after the founder of the competition, American Dwight Davis.

'Davis Cup is both one of the greatest tournaments to play and one of the worst. It's wonderful when you win, but terrible when you lose. I've been more shattered physically and mentally playing Davis Cup than any other event. You're playing for your country, you have a week together as a team, you work tremendously hard to peak for the match and it's an awful anti-climax afterwards. The disappointment is dreadful if you've lost as well,' John said.

He and David Lloyd were the mainstay of the Britain's Davis Cup squad in the seventies and their most memorable matches – and one of the most glorious in British Davis Cup history – came when they played doubles against Italy in July 1976 at Wimbledon. The two brothers were the heroes of an epic three hour fifty-two minute match against Adriano Panatta and Paolo Bertolucci whom they eventually beat 6–8, 3–6, 6–3, 18–16, 6–2 (there being no tie-breakers in the Davis Cup), having been match point-down five times.

'It changed the face of British tennis; it was something I'll never forget,' David said.

John Barrett remembers that John was a considerable asset as a team member although he tended to skimp on the practice sessions. 'He was very easy on a team except that he found it awfully difficult to graft in practice. The really great players are the ones who can really push themselves to the limits in practice. When John was thirteen he used to push himself, but of course he wasn't then playing a lot of matches.

'Roy Emerson, for example (the Australian Wimbledon champion in 1964 and 1965), was an absolute tiger on the court as a junior – he would chase balls that were well out just to give himself the exercise and the experience of being overstretched and still making a shot. But John would run to a point, see the ball was going out and let it go. He wouldn't push himself. Nor would he recover his equilibrium after two or three bad shots running; he would want to stop and would say, "I can't play; to hell with it, what's the point?" If he wasn't timing everything perfectly then he thought it wasn't worth the effort. We tried to rationalize all this with him. He would accept both criticism and advice quite readily, but he didn't always find it easy to put them into practice. He was a frustrating person to be working with because you could see how much talent he had.'

Fellow players remember that John would practise if it was convenient but not if the courts were the other side of town – 'too much aggro,' he'd complain, and not bother to go.

Home for John was a flat he'd bought in Edgehill, Wimbledon where he settled happily into a life-style of takeaway food from Wimbledon restaurants and many hours in front of the television. 'His friends knew not to try to engage him in conversation until the last dot had vanished from the screen,' Peter Risdon, a close friend of John's, remembered.

He was also turning into quite a star, being both one of the best British players and by far the most good looking. He became a sporting idol, very much in demand by starlets, models and actresses in his favourite nightime haunt, the discothèque Tramp in the centre of London. Actress Susan George was one girlfriend, and Valerie Perrine another. The latter, to John's considerable embarrassment, turned up at Wimbledon to watch him in a chauffeur-driven white Rolls-Royce once.

John rather enjoyed the star-studded high life, whereas brother David disapproved of the fact that John featured so much in gossip columns and thought it gave him a bad image. But John used to tease fellow Davis Cup player Buster Mottram because his press coverage was more than Buster's. In return, Buster nick-named John 'Mr Convenience' since he disliked travelling to Italy and Spain because of the difficulty of trying to obtain taxis, practice courts and so on in foreign languages, and the Latin disorganization. At home, John was so amiable that he could escape with a lot. He couldn't drive so he was always trying to get lifts from people. 'He got away with it when no one else would because he was so nice,' John Feaver said.

John was excused almost any misdemeanour, even when he once, rather dumbly, packed his passport in his suitcase and checked it in on the way to a Galea Cup match. The case had to be retrieved and the Lloyd passport unpacked before the plane could take off.

Chris was also enjoying her share of famous escorts and went out with actor Burt Reynolds and Jack Ford, the son of President Ford. She remembers that neither were very serious boyfriends: 'I wasn't looking for a relationship; I was looking for companionship, someone to go out with. I really liked them a lot but I never considered a future with them. Sometimes I didn't see them for a month then we'd meet during my week off from the tour.'

Even though they'd broken off their engagement, Chris remained very fond of Jimmy Connors. 'I still carried a torch for him. I went out with other men but I thought about him for two or three years after we broke up. I saw him at tournaments, and we went out in between his girlfriends and my boyfriends. He was still number one with me right up until I met John. It's hard to get that first love out of your system. I still hoped something would happen and Jimmy and I would get back together again.'

Their meetings tended sometimes to be awkward because they'd never formally finished the affair: 'We never had that face-to-face talk when you say, "I still care for you and good luck in whatever you do."'

It wasn't until Jimmy had married Patti and Chris had married John – both in 1979 – that they laughingly discussed their romance. 'Jimmy told me that I'd been too tough on him, that I was too possessive, and I told him that he had too much of a roving eye,' Chris said.

Chris was very badly hurt by Jimmy flaunting his girlfriends, particularly when he turned up in the Players' Box at Wimbledon during Chris's 1975 semi-final against Billie Jean King with actress Susan George in tow.

'I didn't see them but afterwards I was told they were right in the front row watching me,' Chris said. 'It was a desperate thing to do, very inconsiderate, but then men don't think terribly carefully.'

Chris's life on the circuit for the first few years after she turned pro was solid tennis. 'I was very protected; I concentrated on practising and playing my matches. I wasn't really aware of other people, I just saw them on the side but I wasn't sociable. I was the quiet type, and spent a lot of time in my hotel room, eating room service meals, watching television, listening to music and reading books.'

Ingrid Bentzer gave a vivid picture of life on the women's circuit which was anything but glamorous in middle America in the dead of winter.

'Often you wake up and have no idea where you are. When you've played a late match you go back to the hotel and the restaurant is shut so you have to make do with room service. You're too "high" to sleep so you try to unwind by watching television or playing Scrabble. I said to Chris once, "Let's go shopping," but she was busy and she said, "Tomorrow I'm playing singles, the next day doubles, then I'm giving an interview – how about an hour next week?" When we finally made it, it felt like Christmas. It's impossible to get laundry done or your shoes mended before you move on.'

The lifestyle resembles that of an office worker except that the office is constantly moving round the world and players commute to it by plane. That's how Arthur Ashe saw his life: he used to stroll off court whistling and joking, 'Just another day at the office.'

Overseas, Chris was still fairly oblivious of her surroundings. 'When I went to the French Open my goal wasn't to see Paris, it was to win the tournament. It meant getting up, practising, showering, having a massage; everything focussed on winning the match. Going shopping on the Champs Elysée, to parties or to discos were a distraction and I never did any of them. There were also a lot of demands on top players' time. When we had a day off we had to do press interviews, work for our endorsements or fulfil Women's Tennis Association commitments so we didn't have much free time. It was different for the middle and lower ranked players, but I was pretty single-minded. It was almost as if I had a fear that if I had fun it would distract me and detract from my game. Sounds terrible, doesn't it?'

It took Chris some time to thaw the frostiness with which she'd been greeted on the women's circuit initially, and getting accepted as one of 'the girls' was a slow business. Ana Leaird saw the gap: 'All the older girls were travelling alone, smoking cigarettes and drinking beer, and Chris was so much younger and escorted by her mother. They didn't know how to relate to her nor she to them.'

Once Chris started to travel by herself, when she was nineteen, the atmosphere changed and she became particular friends with Billie Jean King, Rosie Casals and several of the other players.

'Billie Jean had great leadership qualities and she was a marvellous spokeswoman for women's tennis. She's the reason why the game took off – she had a dream and made it happen. She was one of the greatest match players ever. When I think of ambitious and feisty players she comes to mind first.'

Rosie Casals was also one of Chris's closest friends. 'She's so giving and has such an infectious sense of fun. I think that may have prevented her from becoming an even greater player. She's great; you'd often see her in the locker room after a match having a beer and a cigarette.'

For someone from such a narrow background Chris wasn't bothered by the lesbianism on the circuit. 'Whenever a lot of women are thrown together part of the group is likely to be gay. I never felt threatened by the fact that some of the girls who I really liked – and who were good friends – were; it didn't bother me at all. I am not, but I never judged them on it,' she said.

Some of Chris's opponents found it hard to understand that she could fool around and be friendly in the locker room then switch to a ruthlessness on court. Ana Leaird, who travelled with Chris frequently between 1973 and 1975, explained that Chris would psych herself up to a winning mentality by pre-match tantrums and bad temper.

'Before a match she could be a bitch; that's the only way I can describe it. If I said to her in the morning, "Do you want tea or coffee?" she'd snap back, "I've told you three times I want coffee." Then I'd know she was going to win 6–2, 6–2. Sometimes I could tell she was going to lose simply because she was being too nice.'

Afterwards Chris would feel guilty and generously go out and buy the victims of her moodiness a present to prove she didn't mean it.

'It would bother her, even though she knew she had to do it,' Ana said. 'I used to tell her that I couldn't hit balls with her or talk strategy but I could be with her and let her scream at me. That was my contribution to helping her get ready for the match.'

Chris turned pro on her eighteenth birthday and was at last able to collect the prize money she won. Her first cheque was for $10,000 at Fort Lauderdale and she said it has sometimes baffled her the amount of money tennis players make.

'When I started playing it was at an amateur level and we played for trophies which was a thrill in itself. Then the prizes graduated to crystal glasses and I would get expense money, too. Sometimes if I played a tournament for a week I got $250 expenses which was a lot of money for us back in those days. I was amazed by the first cheque I won – my life didn't change and I was still playing tennis but I was getting hundreds of thousands of dollars for doing it. Sometimes I felt guilty because I could see my brothers and sisters struggling, putting just as much time into their tennis as I did, but I was the one who was successful. Maybe I had a little more determination and it was meant for me to be the champion. It's very difficult when you see your friends and your family struggling financially, because it's very hard for them to accept your prize money.'

Chris's father formed a corporation, Evert Enterprises Inc, through which he could handle the investment of her winnings, and Chris remembers expounding her fairly conservative investment philosophy to him.

'I don't care if you never make me a penny out of what I've earned but don't lose any of my money. I would much rather you be safe than sorry and we don't want to worry about whether the tax authorities are going to get us so just pay what you have to pay. I think a lot of people have done it the other way and made a lot of money but lost a lot, too.'

Chris gives over a quarter of the corporation's income to her family and is the first to credit them for their substantial input into her success.

'My family have worked for me in a sense so they deserve everything they've got. My mother comes with me to about ten tournaments a year and really helps out, and until John and I started to work with Dennis Ralston, my dad was my coach. Even now I never let anyone else string my rackets, and he gets them from Wilson unstrung. Sometimes he'll change the grips, and if a handle is too big he'll take the grip off and shave it.

'When I go to Europe for eight weeks I go over with about eight rackets to start with and then Mom and other people bring over replacements. I usually get through about six a week.'

Not only does Chris prefer her father to do the stringing but she sees it as the most sensible and economical way. 'Every country has different machines and they never get it right. Sometimes you have to have several rackets restrung until finally the tension and tightness are right. It's a process of trial and error, which just seems like a waste of gut to me,' Chris said.

Chris has made millions of dollars during her career. Recently she has earned an annual average of $500,000 in tournament prize money, $500,000 from exhibition matches and special events and another $2 million in endorsements from her major sponsors, Wilson rackets, Ellesse clothes, Converse shoes, Lipton's Tea, Cirrus Banking Systems, Rolex, British Airways, Bovril and contracts in Japan.

Her first extravagant purchase was a lynx coat when she was twenty-one, which turned out to be a very good investment. 'I bought it for $4,000 and now it's worth about $15,000,' Chris said.

She is inordinately generous to her family and friends but not a big spender personally. 'I think it's due to my upbringing when I was taught that materialism is evil and to avoid temptations. I'm a bit like my Dad in that respect. He would always tell us stories about living through the Depression and the war, eating a lot of canned food because fresh meat was a luxury, and it makes you think. I would have no problems buying my mother a Jaguar or a Mercedes or anything for my family, but I'm not really extravagant when it comes to myself.'

Mrs Evert worried about the effects of Chris's generosity on her brothers and sisters. 'I had to speak to her once because I didn't want the kids to get completely spoilt. If you have too much at an early age then there's nothing to look forward to. Since then she has always checked with me whether it's all right for her to give so and so this or that.'

Both the Evert parents have enjoyed her success in different ways. Mrs Evert has been the one who has shared the travelling while Mr Evert has only been to one Wimbledon and three US Opens because of work commitments and a high blood pressure problem, but he thinks the world of Chris.

'You can just look into Jimmy's eyes and see how proud he is of her as a player and a person. He doesn't enjoy the travelling, and he's happy in his home. He really is a saint, so humble and good. He's enjoying her success to the utmost but not in a way which is obvious,' Mrs Evert said.

The Everts have always been careful not to lavish all their attention on Chris because she was the superstar, and have been meticulous about making sure the others didn't feel left out. Drew got a tennis scholarship to the University of Alabama before becoming a tennis pro at Amelia Island; Jeanne supervises the Women's Tennis Association clinics for aspiring players and is married to Brahm Dubin who manages the Boca Greens Country Club in Florida. John got a tennis scholarship to Vanderbilt University and now works for IMG; and Clare graduates in 1985 and is going to Southern University in Dallas, Texas.

'Jimmy and I have always felt even more obligated to the other children because of Chrissie's success,' Mrs Evert said.

Chris still stays at home with her parents for the weeks in January and February when she plays tournaments in Florida, and is picked up without fuss or VIP treatment at Miami airport by Clare and boyfriend, Ray, signing autographs for fans who recognize her as she waits for them to bring the car round. During the drive home Chris twiddles with the radio wavebands and catches up on the latest pop hits and fashions with Clare, a vivacious and attractive teenager. 'She keeps me in touch,' laughs Chris, who is extremely fond of and gets along famously with her little sister.

It was Chris who, with her father and John, jumped into a car to go and pick up Clare after a minor car crisis when her own car was undriveable.

She'll gently rib her father over dinner when he suggests that the amount Chris and John drive their cars it may have been preferable to have leased them. 'Dad, how much money have I earned in total?'

Both of her parents still get terribly nervous watching Chris play. Mrs Evert has a reputation at Wimbledon for being a chain-smoker and fraught until Chris has built up a comfortable lead. Mr Evert doesn't even relax then. During his only visit to Wimbledon in 1975 Chris was leading 6–2, 3–0 in the semi-final against Billie Jean King and one of her friends remarked to him, 'It's all over.'

He cautioned, 'Don't be so sure,' and sure enough Billie Jean went on to win. Usually he watches Chris's matches at home on television and will wander away from the screen for a few seconds if things get too tense.

Mrs Evert still rates as one of her worst frights – but a very funny experience in retrospect – when she thought she'd missed one of Chris's matches altogether. During a rainy Wimbledon on a day when it looked highly unlikely that Chris would be playing, Mrs Evert took the train up to London to do some shopping. Catching a glimpse of a television screen in a shop window in Regent Street she was horrified to see Chris on court. 'Daggers went through my heart,' she remembers. She peered in again and, as only a mother would, looked to see what Chris was wearing. Relief swept over her as she saw it was last year's dress and realized a re-run of the previous year's match was being shown.

The Evert household doesn't revolve around Chris, which is the way they all like it. Mrs Evert says: 'Chris has never had an exalted view of herself. In our family she wouldn't have got away with it; the wind would have been taken out of her sails if she'd started bragging, but she was never that type. All this success didn't overwhelm us, and I don't think we were mesmerized by her. She's still normal and human.'

John became a household name at Wimbledon in 1977 when he beat no. 4 seed, Roscoe Tanner, who'd been a semi-finalist in 1975 and 1976, 3–6, 6–4, 6–4, 8–6. John had already beaten him the previous year in the Pacific South-West Championships in California 1–6, 6–2, 7–6 where he had gone on to beat the 1972 Wimbledon champion, Stan Smith before losing to Arthur Ashe in the quarter-finals.

But it was John's phenomenal match against Tanner on the opening day of Wimbledon which ensured a place for him, and his nicknames of 'Flossie' and 'Legs', in the newspaper headlines. (A fellow junior player, Stanley Matthews, had dubbed him 'Flossie' because of his long hair. The nickname still confuses Americans who try and work out its association with dental floss.)

The following day John had to have a police escort from the

dressing-room to the court for his second-round match against German Karl Meiler, and he learnt the transient nature of victory when he had a let-down and lost.

'I did so many press interviews after the Tanner match and people were phoning me up all night saying "Great Match", "Congratulations", and "Wonderful News". I woke up the next day absolutely exhausted and lost a match I ought to have won,' John said.

Wimbledon was just one tournament in an outstanding year for John. In the autumn he lost to Bjorn Borg – whom he had beaten the year before in Monte Carlo – in the finals of the Swiss Open in Basle. He met him in November in the finals of the Benson and Hedges tournament at Wembley, and lost again.

His third major final in a few months was the Australian Open in Kooyong, Melbourne in December. John had only gone to Australia in an attempt to get on to the bonus board and so collect the payments which players who end the year at the top of the ATP computer rankings get. It turned out that he played his finest Grand Slam ever.

'I knew that I needed to win one round in Sydney and one in Melbourne. That's what I was aiming for, and I didn't think I had any chance of doing really well.'

John's first hurdle in the Open draw was the suave, confident Australian John Newcombe – one of the favourites to win. 'He had an unbelievable image, and was a huge star. The crowd used to shout out the catch phrase, "Beauty Newk" all the time, and he'd tipped himself to win the title that year,' John said. But John played marvellous tennis to cause an upset, 6–0, 5–7, 6–4. He went on to beat another Australian, Bob Giltinan, in the semi-finals to become the first British player since Fred Perry in 1934 to reach the men's singles final of the Australian Open. His opponent was Vitas Gerulaitis, with whom he'd been practising all week. 'Playing Vitas was like playing a friend,' John said, and many say that was what cost him the title.

John should have won and was very close to doing so. Vitas won the first two sets, 6–3, 7–6. John took the third 7–5 and at 2–all in the fourth Vitas was crippled with cramp. John took that set but played tentatively to lose the fifth set and the match. Commentators pointed to his lack of killer instinct in not being able to defeat a cramp-afflicted opponent, but John defended the way he played. 'I changed my tactics because I thought it was the best thing to do at the time.'

John's father is among those who maintain that had he won it would have given John a boost and a breakthrough which would have made an enormous difference to his entire career, but John is less sure.

'I would have got more contracts and made more money in the short term; I would have got a higher ranking and more prestige. I'd had three finals in a row and was no. 24 in the world, so should have strived for the next big step, getting into the top ten, but I didn't. I worked a little bit harder but was content to be around that mark and that was a weakness.'

One of the ironies was that John had beaten Vitas in straight sets 7–6, 6–3 when they'd first played against each other five years before in the under-21 international team competition for the BP Cup after trailing 1–3 in both sets. John Barrett saw the match: 'He beat Vitas on merit. But by the time they met at Kooyong Vitas had already passed him and was a highly ranked world player. John wasn't; he'd never gone on.'

John flew back from Australia to a press conference at Queen's Club. After it, John Barrett and Paul Hutchins congratulated him warmly on his success but also tried to convince him that he must use his great achievement as a launchpad to go on to greater things – to win rather than be runner-up.

'We told him that then was the moment to start,' John Barrett remembered. 'But I'm afraid he never did take off from there. The press conference was in the card room at Queen's Club and I remember thinking as the tennis deities looked down from their portraits, "If only their sort of ambition could be instilled in a player with this sort of talent." It worried me that he seemed to be satisfied with what he'd achieved so far.'

Although John had missed the tennis victory which would have changed the course of his tennis career, at Wimbledon six months later he was to meet the girl who would ensure that his life would never be the same again.

CHAPTER FOUR

1978
A Wimbledon Romance

The queue outside the transportation office of the All England Club, Wimbledon wasn't a particularly promising place for the start of a romance between the ice maiden of tennis, Chris Evert, and Britain's golden boy of the courts, John Lloyd. But this is where they were introduced to each other for the first time, by a mutual friend, Ingrid Bentzer, the Swedish no. 1, who was one of the circuit's most popular personalities. They were all waiting for tournament courtesy cars to ferry them back to homes and hotels one summer's evening during the second week of the championship.

John was rather embarrassed although he had been quietly watching Chris for some time and to this day doesn't remember saying much more than just 'hello'. But Chris has more vivid and slightly unfavourable memories of her future husband's first greeting.

'It's lovely to meet you,' John said shyly and Chris immediately thought, 'Oh no, he must be gay,' because she'd never heard the word 'lovely' used by a man before and it rather destroyed the mental image which she'd built up of Britain's Adonis-like glamour boy whom she'd been admiring from afar for some time.

John recalls that Chris, who had never been out with an Englishman, had nevertheless developed some reservations about their masculinity.

It was the unmistakable British accent which had aroused Chris's suspicions: 'I thought Englishmen were a bit feminine because the accent is so beautiful that somehow it sounds more attractive coming from a woman than a man. I just had to get used to the accent; American accents on women sound more masculine but English accents on men are not so masculine because it's such a soft sound.'

However, all was not lost with John. She took one look at him, listened to his less than immortal opening words and thought, 'OK, John, you're fine if you don't talk.' Fine for a date, that was, but no thoughts of marriage crossed her mind.

The couple had in fact almost met several years before at Crystal Palace during a practice session for the Dewar Cup. John was warming up with his brother David when Chris and Rosie Casals came to take over their practice court. John's good looks, which were to intrigue Chris a few years later, made no impact at all at the time.

When her friend, Ana Leaird, who was with Chris and Rosie, gushed, 'Isn't John cute?' Chris quashed her enthusiasm by saying, 'But he's so young.'

Chris, however, made an impression on John and he decided to keep an eye on her, thinking she had a very good figure.

'I always thought she had very classy looks. It's funny that we had never met because I knew probably every girl on the circuit except for her. I had just never been in her circle of friends, and she was not in mine.'

It is an indication of the extent to which the men's and women's tennis circuits had enlarged and separated that Britain's no. 3 player had never met the American no. 1, a situation which would have been highly unlikely a few years before.

Chris was also still regarded as Jimmy Connors's girlfriend. Their relationship had drifted on for the four or so years after they had broken off their engagement in 1974.

John finally caught Chris's attention when she was playing in the women's tournament at Devonshire Park, Eastbourne, which precedes both Queen's Club and Wimbledon, principally through the extensive publicity he generated as a tennis sex-symbol during the few weeks of the year – around Wimbledon – when tennis fever envelopes Britain. In 1978 nearly every newspaper or magazine carried a tennis story accompanied by a photograph of John in various stages of undress staring out of the page.

Chris picked up a magazine in Eastbourne and saw one such feature. 'John was sprawled out in his bathrobe; the headlines were "It's lonely at the top" or something like that. I read the article and thought he sounded a real nice guy, and it opened my eyes a little bit because while I knew most of the players on the circuit I didn't know him at all.'

Chris, who was sharing a suite at the Grand Hotel, Eastbourne, with close friends and fellow players Ingrid Bentzer and Stephanie Tolleson, didn't think further about John until a couple of days later when she walked into the sitting-room and found Stephanie in raptures, her face held inches from the television screen.

'I asked, "Stephanie, are your eyes that bad? What are you doing so close to the TV?" She drooled, "Look at that; isn't he gorgeous?" and there was John Lloyd playing a match. I thought, "Yes, he is cute."'

John attracted yet more publicity at the International Championships at Queen's Club by beating former Australian idol, John Newcombe on 21 June.

'Newk', as he is known, had won the men's singles at Wimbledon in 1967, 1970 and 1971, and John had beaten him in the 1977 Australian Open on his way to the final with Vitas Gerulaitis.

Although Newcombe showed his age in the match it was still a good 6–4, 6–4 win for John who got through to the quarter-finals before losing to American Sandy Mayer, the man who had beaten Ilie Nastase at Wimbledon in 1973.

Keen, no doubt, to feed the public's insatiable appetite for pictures and titbits about their sexy tennis idol, the *Daily Mirror* ran a three-part series on him from 20 to 22 June, along with a mini-exposé of life behind the scenes on the tennis circuit. John and his then-manager, John Barrett, were livid when the tabloid's photographer duped John into having his photo taken without his shirt on, hugging a topless model. It appeared with the caption 'Model partners: being photographed with luscious ladies such as Tessa Hewitt is one of the perks of John Lloyd's job.' The accompanying copy consisted of anecdotes about Ilie Nastase having lost a bet with Vitas Gerulaitis about whether he would drop his trousers in a Puerto Rican restaurant, and other pranks, such as another player's narrow escape from an attractive black model who pursued him. Had they become more intimately acquainted he would have discovered her to be a male.

The *Daily Mirror* became compulsory reading in the men's locker room at Queen's Club that week where it caused much mirth. John was teased mercilessly and word of the revelations soon spread to the women's circuit.

Chris opened a copy of the paper and the topless photo instantly caught her attention – both for the appeal of John's naked chest and the risqué nature of the shot. 'He must be a bit of a raver,' she concluded.

When Chris knew John better and had met Mrs Lloyd, she asked him, 'What did you tell your mother about that photo?'

John said, 'I told her it was superimposed because she'd had the neighbours saying, "Your John wouldn't do that, would he?"' Chris could hardly believe John's audacity and Mrs Lloyd's gullibility.

In the same newspaper series John said that he would like nothing better than to find a steady girlfriend to travel with him and give him stability and companionship on the helter-skelter of the international tennis circuit.

It all sounded very familiar to Chris, because although she had been ranked the no. 1 tennis player in the world for five years she felt unfulfilled. Something was missing. Tennis, success, money and fame were no longer enough, and there was a void in her life. She was also caught in a dilemma about marriage: on the one hand, she felt she wanted to find someone to marry and settle down with; on the other, she had split up from Jimmy Connors because she didn't feel ready for children and the domestic scene. She thought she was too young, too competitive and had too much potential to swop a champion's tennis career for motherhood yet.

Then there was the problem of what sort of person to marry: a high flyer like herself to whom she would have to play a supporting role, to the detriment of her own career, rather than being supported in her own endeavours; or a less forceful personality than herself who would concede her top billing.

The first choice could result in the clash of two ambitions; the second the hang-ups for both partners inherent in a situation where a famous wife eclipses her co-starring husband who, in comparison, appears to be a 'yes man'. Being in the same sport could only be an additional complicating factor. Neither option guaranteed a 'happy ever after' ending. No matter, timing, which determines the success or failure of so many relationships, was on Chris and John's side at Wimbledon in 1978.

John had been out with many starlets, actresses, models and other attractive women and had broken up three months before with the singer Maureen Nolan of the Nolan Sisters group. Although he is now inclined to dismiss the relationship as youthful infatuation, it was serious at the time and he was hurt when it ended. Had it become permanent the logistics of trying to organize concerts and tennis tournaments in nearby venues might soon have proved impossible.

Chris hadn't had a serious relationship since her engagement to Jimmy Connors had ended although she had dated Vitas Gerulaitis, Jack Ford and Burt Reynolds. Her relationship with Connors was not progressing, so she had started to look around for alternative boyfriends. Who better than the dashing, blue-eyed John Lloyd of tabloid notoriety?

That Wimbledon in 1978 Chris, trying to sound casual, asked Ingrid whether she knew John: 'Oh yes, he's a friend of mine,' came the reply. Chris was nonplussed: 'You didn't tell me that before,' she said, peeved that Ingrid hadn't mentioned her acquaintance with this gorgeous male who she was trying to meet. 'What's he like?' she enquired, trying to disguise her eagerness to find out more about him. 'He's very nice; different to other tennis players,' Ingrid said. Chris asked Ingrid whether she could introduce her to John, reluctant to approach him directly herself.

Ingrid needed little encouragement and, besides, she thought that Chris and John would be very compatible. Having watched them glancing at each other on the sun-roof of the players' tea-room for a week, she felt that it was about time someone took the initiative. Choosing her time, she approached John in the tea-room, chatted to him and got swiftly to the point.

'Chris's a nice, interesting girl,' she told John. 'Why don't you go and talk to her?'

'Pardon me?' spluttered a startled John, his cool completely deserting him. 'I don't even know her. What would I talk to her about?'

When faced with a superstar such as Chris, John was even more reluctant than usual to use either his fame or his sex appeal to his advantage and took some persuading.

'I've never been the sort of person to just walk up cold and say, "Hello, how are you?" I just can't do it, I have to be introduced. I've never been that brash,' he said.

And even though Chris was a star she wasn't the type of girl to arrange to bump into John nor approach him and introduce herself. 'As confident as I was in my tennis, I was very shy with men. I've always been very shy. All the dates I've had with well-known people were set up.'

Nevertheless, after Ingrid's brief introduction outside the Wimbledon transportation office it was very much left to Chris to make the next move. She went back to Ingrid the next day and said, 'I think John's really neat – do you think you can set up a date or arrange for us all to go out somewhere?' Ingrid agreed to mention it to him, and she is the type of person who, when asked to carry out a plan, does it.

John found himself on the receiving end of Ingrid's matchmaking designs once again.

'She came up and said, "A couple of the girls and I want to go to a night-club; which one do you recommend?"

'I said, "Tramp is the best place."'

'But we're not members,' Ingrid replied, fishing, and John took the bait.

'I'll get you in,' he volunteered. 'Who's going?'

'Stephanie, Chris and I,' said Ingrid.

'I got very nervous about that, obviously,' John recalled later. He mentioned the proposed date to his mother who had come to Wimbledon that day to give him her opinion about a town-house he was thinking of buying. When John said he was in two minds about whether to join Ingrid and her friends Mrs Lloyd advised him to go along, little realizing what it would lead to.

It wasn't the fact that Chris was a celebrity which caused John's unease. It was rather that she was something of an enigma to the male tennis players. 'She never featured in the dressing-room gossip,' John remembered. 'She'd always gone out with Jimmy and he wasn't a big socializer with the other players. I wondered what I was going to say to her. It was like going on a blind date with someone I didn't know how to react to. I'd read all the press coverage of her so I thought she'd be cold and I could imagine us both staring at each other not knowing what to say. That's what I was nervous about.'

In fact John almost missed the date altogether. Chris, in dressy white trousers and a white shirt, arrived at Tramp on time at ten o'clock with Ingrid and Stephanie, who was feeling very sick but had been inveigled into the outing by Chris. They were standing just inside the front doors of the club, feeling a bit put out because John wasn't there to greet them. At 10.15 Chris elected to give him five more minutes then leave because loitering conspicuously in the foyer looking as though they had been stood up wasn't a comfortable experience for any of them.

Meanwhile John, preened for the date and resplendent in white suit, was fraught, sitting in his Wimbledon maisonette and drumming his fingers on the table because the taxi he had ordered hadn't shown up. 'I was desperately phoning the car-hire firm every two minutes. It was getting later and later, and I was really sweating. Though I had been nervous of meeting her, once the date was arranged I had really begun to look forward to it.'

The car finally arrived and after a record-breaking journey to Tramp in Jermyn Street off Piccadilly John raced in to find the girls still there. Composing himself he reflected, 'What a start!'

John quickly found a table and ordered a round of drinks. He and Chris began to chat and, contrary to his expectations that it would take some time to break the ice, they hit it off within the first ten minutes.

'I was in shock,' John remembered. 'I felt as if I'd known her for five or ten years. It was such a pleasure to realize that so much which had been written about her was rubbish. She was extremely warm and very quick, really on the ball. Here was this girl who was supposed to be cold and shy – although she's shy in some ways – with a wicked sense of humour, telling loads of jokes. I was intrigued by that right away.'

Something clicked for Chris, too. After romances with a tennis ace, a Hollywood star and the son of the President of the United States, it seemed as though she had found a soul-mate who, in the cut-throat world of top international tennis, still managed to keep his feet firmly on the ground. Her feelings were almost ones of relief.

'We had each gone out with other people before but we knew we were really only trying to find someone like ourselves. I think that's when I realized I'd found a man with a similar family background, morals and way of thinking,' said Chris. 'The men I'd been out with in the past had all been high-powered and ambitious. With my being in such a competitive field they always felt that they had something to prove. John was the other extreme. He was the first guy I'd met who had everything in the right perspective. He enjoyed life and seemed to be at peace with himself; he was a real gentle person.

'It had been exciting with the others but it had been a pain in the neck for a lot of the time. I wasn't sure if that up and down feeling was what I wanted for the rest of my life.'

Chris realized that she differed from John's previous girlfriends. 'In his eyes I was a little more aggressive compared to English women, and had more drive. I cracked jokes, too.'

After half-an-hour or so Stephanie started to feel more sick and retired back to her hotel. Chris, who was reluctant to be seen alone with John by the press, asked Ingrid to stay to make them appear an innocent threesome but soon John and Chris were totally absorbed with each other's company. When Ingrid returned to her seat from the dance floor and said something to them neither replied, so seeing that the date she had masterminded was progressing so well, she also went home.

John and Chris talked in Tramp until the early hours when he gave her a lift back to the Inn on the Park. He didn't kiss her goodnight but since the evening had gone so well he summoned up the courage to ask her for a second date.

Chris told him that she would like to see him again but cautioned that they would have to be very discreet. She had learnt her lesson about conducting affairs in the full glare of publicity four years before when photographers and gossip columnist scouts shadowed her and Jimmy Connors everywhere they went.

'We'll go to a quiet restaurant,' John promised. The next day he sought the advice of one of his man-about-town friends for the name of a suitably secluded place and booked a table for a few nights later at Newton's at the far, unfashionable end of the King's Road, in the opposite direction to Alexander's, a Chelsea haunt much patronized by the tennis set.

Meanwhile the friendship continued furtively at Wimbledon during the tournament. Anxious to avoid the gossips on the tennis circuit who delight in detecting the tell-tale signs of assignations between players, Chris and John resorted to the rather juvenile method of communication, sign language.

Raised eyebrows from John in the Wimbledon tea-room meant, 'Meet me on the rooftop balcony', where they would then keep a discreet distance pretending not to notice each other. While ostensibly studying the action on courts 2 and 3 below, they would exchange a few words. During one such rooftop liaison they looked down to see a gaggle of Fleet Street photographers so they immediately fled in opposite directions.

Their second date, the night before Chris's singles final with Martina Navratilova, started nervously with Chris and John very anxious lest someone recognize them. 'Don't worry,' John said, trying to allay Chris's fears by telling her that Newtons wasn't a restaurant frequented by players and the tennis groupies. They relaxed and were soon chatting animatedly, enjoying their meal of fish, when suddenly John heard the unmistakable laugh of Lennart Bergelin, Bjorn Borg's coach, who swept down the stairs with a group of players, press and officials including Bjorn's future wife, Mariana Simionescu. Chris and John stared down at their plates and held their breath, hoping that they wouldn't be recognized. Luckily they weren't.

'Of all the restaurants in London we had to choose the same one,' John breathed out after the near miss, sure that Chris would think he was an idiot. He paid the bill as fast as he could and they left.

John and Chris returned to her hotel and John suggested that they should enjoy the glorious summer's evening with a walk in Hyde Park before they said goodnight. But the romance of this moonlit stroll was interrupted by a bizarre display by one of the eccentrics who hang out in parks at night-time the world over. The man yelled and screamed, swinging from the branches of the trees and at one point Chris and John thought they might be attacked. It was with a certain amount of relief, after this unsettling experience, that the couple got back to the hotel.

It had been an evening of near misses – they'd avoided detection by the Swedes and molestation in Hyde Park – John thought as he said goodnight. He wished Chris good luck for the final the following day and hastily departed without so much as a goodnight peck on the cheek.

The next time he saw her was on the Centre Court playing well against Martina Navratilova in the women's singles final. The score in the first set was 2–all but Martina failed to win another game and Chris secured it 6–2. Martina won the second set and was leading 2–0 in the third when Chris swiftly went on the attack and came back to a 4–2 lead.

John, who was sitting in the players' enclosure with Martin Hill, an old friend from junior tennis circuit days, could barely contain his excitement. 'Chris's going to win,' he nudged Martin, fidgeting with anticipation, 'It'll be a great night tonight; we can go out and celebrate.'

Within minutes, however, there was one of those changes of fortunes on court which make tennis so riveting – Martina levelled at 4–all in the third set. Although Chris had a 5–4 lead she couldn't beat off the buoyant Czech's final challenging burst, and minutes later Chris was shaking hands with Martina at the net – as the loser, not the victor.

Chris was scheduled to go back to the United States the following day and John was abruptly woken from his daydreams of a celebratory evening to the realization that their second date the previous evening might have been their last. Intense disappointment engulfed him and he remembers, 'I was really upset.' Turning to Martin he said despondently, 'Well, obviously that's the last time we'll get to see each other because she won't want to go out tonight. I don't blame her.'

Chris put her defeat down to her new relationship with John. It wasn't that she had spent all her time looking towards him instead of keeping her eye on the ball, nor that every time she tossed up the ball to serve she could only think of him, but rather that she was filled with an intense feeling of happiness because she'd just met someone right, who had added an extra dimension to her life, and this had diluted the normal hunger she would have brought to a Wimbledon final.

In the locker room the telephone rang. Chris, just out of the shower, took the call: it was Ingrid, who had flown to Amsterdam the previous day, ringing to console her, but Chris sounded much less depressed than Ingrid had expected. Instead of gloomily rehashing the match, Chris told her excitedly that she was seeing John that night.

Later Chris admitted that she surprised herself with such behaviour which differed from her usual routine after losing a match. 'Normally I would have gone straight home rather than putting on my jeans and going up to the tea-room to socialize. But I wasn't feeling too miserable, so I went up and sat with some of the other players.' Australians Tony Roche, Fred Stolle and Lew Hoad tried to talk her into having a beer but Chris, who detests it, did at least settle for a shandy.

The closeness and magic John had felt across the dinner table the night before – at least until the Swedes arrived – were now forgotten as he hovered awkwardly on the opposite side of the tea-room, confused about the best course of action for the very new boyfriend of a defeated Wimbledon finalist.

'I had no idea how she would react, but I thought she would probably not want to go out. I knew I had to leave the next morning and I had visions of our brief relationship finishing right there. I thought that at least I had to try and say goodbye.'

Eventually he summoned up the courage and tentatively approached Chris, who introduced him to Mrs Evert. She was immediately attracted by the kindness in his eyes and liked him from the start. She put him at his ease by chatting and smiling just as if Chris had won. Feeling gauche, John managed to find a few words to say to Chris.

'Bad luck,' he murmured. 'Do you still want to go out tonight? I understand perfectly if you don't.'

'You bet I do!' Chris replied instantly. Having lost a Wimbledon crown because of her new love, she didn't now intend to have the date with the object of her affections cancelled.

However, the third date between the teeny boppers' idol, who had to have a police escort in and out of the Wimbledon dressing-rooms, and the eligible superstar wasn't a sophisticated dinner at the best table in a fashionable restaurant, late night revelling at a star-studded party or a twirl around the dance floor at Tramp followed by a night of passion.

Old loyalties for Chris still took precedence over the new man in her life, so first she had a straightforward room-service dinner at the Inn on the Park with her ex-lover Jimmy Connors, who was due to play Bjorn Borg in the men's finals the following day. It was a matter of long-term friendship for her – and support, too.

The beginning of Chris and John's relationship differed from the start of her affair with Jimmy when she'd fallen head over heels in love. 'My relationship with John grew out of a friendship. Jimmy and I fell in love and were attracted to each other before we developed a deep understanding and became friends, but with John it was the reverse,' Chris said.

Although their affair was over Chris was more tactful about his feelings than he had been about hers when he'd flaunted his new girlfriends – models, Miss World or actress Susan George – around Wimbledon. During their long on-off relationship she had rarely gone out with other men unless Jimmy had first told her that he was seeing someone else, when she followed suit.

'Since it was the night before probably one of the biggest matches of his life I didn't want to rock the boat. Seeing John was the first time during my relationship with Jimmy that I felt I was doing something behind his back. During those four years he had shown me many times that I was important in his life so I felt that while I had finally met a great guy, I didn't want to upset Jimmy and cause him to lose his final.

'Jimmy and I still helped each other a lot with our tennis. He used to hit with me and watch my matches and I watched his. We still cared for each other. I felt in a way that I was doing a good deed that evening.'

After Chris had finished having dinner with Jimmy, she met John. The thought of gossip about their young relationship being splashed all over the papers deterred them from making a return visit to Tramp, and John, who was very worried about the prospect of meeting either Mrs Evert or Jimmy who were staying on the same floor as Chris at the Inn on the Park, vetoed meeting Chris in her room. They decided to go to the adjacent Hilton Hotel instead. However, rather than going to any of the bars, or even the coffee shop, they sat and talked for hours in the hotel lobby. As the night wore on the place emptied but John and Chris didn't realize how late it was until the dawn shift of cleaners arrived and they had to keep picking up their feet to avoid a succession of vacuum cleaners.

It was an unromantic episode in the love story the world would dub a fairytale when it got to hear about it but Prince Charming was making a slow start – John, the sexy idol of the courts, was not living up to his image. 'After our third date I was frustrated because John hadn't even tried to kiss me,' said Chris. 'So when we said goodbye I went up to him and hugged him and I think I gave him a quick kiss on the lips. I knew it was up to me to make a move.'

Five months later they announced their engagement.

CHAPTER FIVE

1978-9
Marriage, Honeymoon and Tennis

There was no formal proposal of marriage as such, merely a whispered suggestion from John while he was standing with Chris at the rear of the American team's box at the Royal Albert Hall during the Wightman Cup in November 1978. 'Wouldn't it be funny if we were to phone up our parents and tell them that we were getting married?' he said.

'Yes, why don't we?' agreed Chris, who recognized this as being as near as she was going to get to a proposal, having by then got used to John's shy ways and his slightly casual conduct of their affair. They agreed to keep their plans secret and not announce their engagement until Chris's birthday on 21 December.

John had met Chris's mother briefly in the tea-room at the All England Club at Wimbledon that summer but hadn't met Mr Evert yet so Chris telephoned him at home in Florida though she toned down the message. 'Dad, I want you to meet John; we're quite serious,' she told him.

'I'd really like to meet him,' her father replied in his own low-key way.

The informality of the proposal was compensated for by the grandeur of the setting – the Royal Albert Hall in Kensington with its imposing 10,000-pipe organ and tiers of ornate boxes. It was being used for the Wightman Cup for the first time that year.

Wightman Cup evenings in the Albert Hall have subsequently become an excuse for spirited displays of patriotic fervour – flag-waving and foot-stamping by the thousands of fans who crowd into the lofty arena. Champagne corks pop as the more affluent dinner-jacketed spectators dine grandly in the expensive boxes. The umpire's 'Quiet please' goes unheeded and the noise of clinking glasses and massed knives and forks hitting plates is one of the eccentricities of the occasion.

Even Chris, who made her Wightman Cup debut in 1971 and who hasn't lost a single match in all her appearances there, still finds it a difficult venue, both because of the noise and the sense of being hemmed-in by the steeply rising tiers of boxes. This year there was added excitement. She beat Sue Barker and Virginia Wade in her singles rubbers, but they defeated her and Pam Shriver in the doubles final to give Great Britain the Cup for only the tenth time in the tournament's fifty-year history.

Before Chris returned to the United States later on in November John took her down to Leigh-on-Sea for a day to meet his parents for the first time, an occasion which Mrs Lloyd remembers anticipating nervously. However, even a grey autumn day and an interminable taxi ride from London couldn't dampen Chris's spirits. During the journey John warned her that his father wouldn't be able to stop talking about tennis and that his mother would be a nervous wreck. But Chris soon charmed her future in-laws with her natural friendly nature and lively sense of humour. Mr Lloyd gave her a tour of John's childhood haunts and took her to meet John's elder sister Anne, her husband Bob and their children in their nearby bungalow.

At lunch, with the knack most parents have of embarrassing their children when they don't know whether their relationships are serious or not, Mr Lloyd launched into a little speech. 'I don't want you to think we're putting any pressure on you,' he said, 'but if things progress as they seem to be doing we'll all be very happy.' Remembering this on the way back to London gave Chris an attack of the giggles, and she also wondered if John's mother had liked her because she thought she hadn't looked her in the eye all day. 'Yes, yes, she was just nervous,' reassured John.

He didn't tell his parents that day that he and Chris planned to get married although Mr and Mrs Lloyd suspected something because he hadn't taken many of his other girlfriends home.

But soon the newspaper gossip columnists had discovered the romance and the couple took evasive action, becoming so cautious about what they said that few suspected the couple were as serious about each other as they really were.

After Wimbledon, where the affair had started, it had developed in a series of monstrously expensive phone calls between Chris, who had returned to the United States to fulfil Team Tennis obligations, and John, who was in Europe playing Davis Cup and other tournaments.

The three inconclusive first dates in London had left John out of his depth, in a dither about how to proceed with an affair with the world's no. 1 tennis player. Chris, however, had had no such reservations and all the telephoning was her idea.

'I wanted to keep in close contact with him because I didn't want to lose him. We both travelled about so much and I thought he might forget me in three weeks. I wanted to be assured that he was still thinking about me.'

At the US Open in Flushing Meadow, New York, in September they met again and became lovers. Their stolen nights together were shrouded in the secrecy which had marked their earlier dates at Wimbledon. Chris was staying in the Sheraton while John was staying in a smaller hotel down the road so he did all the commuting.

'I had to sneak in late at night. We had room service dinner then went to bed and I crept out at 6.30 the following morning because Mrs Evert was staying in the same hotel and would not have approved.' Despite such inauspicious beginnings their friendship was deepening into something more serious.

Luckily, nights of passion and little sleep didn't seem to interfere with their tennis.

The draw for the US Open had leading British players Buster Mottram and John playing each other, which resulted in a 6-1,

3–6, 6–1 victory for John, his first ever senior victory over an old rival. In the second round he beat South African, Ray Moore before being put out by the no. 8 seed, Raul Ramirez in the third.

Chris progressed through to the quarter-finals where she defeated up-and-coming teenager Tracy Austin 7–5, 6–1. Tracy's coach, Robert Lansdorp, analysed: 'What Tracy does well, Chris does better; that's the problem.' But Tracy was on the ascent.

Chris disposed of Australian Wendy Turnbull in the semi-finals and then lanky sixteen-year-old Pam Shriver, 7–5, 6–4 in the final. Pam had made a big impact in the tournament, defeating Martina Navratilova in a major upset in a semi-final match which was twice interrupted by rain and tense to the end of the second set tie-breaker, in which Martina saved three match points with fierce winners before going down 7–3.

It was Chris's fourth consecutive US Open crown and she became the first women's winner at Flushing Meadow, the new home of the Open built on the site of the old World Trade Centre in Queen's and adjacent to La Guardia airport outside New York.

The following month John had a foretaste of just how tricky it was going to be playing support role to Chris and doing justice to his own tennis commitments, when he elected to remain in the United States and watch Chris in the finals of a tournament in Bloomington, Minnesota, instead of assembling with the other Davis Cup team members – brother David, Buster Mottram, Mark Cox and Richard Lewis – in Surrey to train for a crucial semi-final against Australia at Crystal Palace in London.

He remembers telling team captain, Paul Hutchins, on the telephone from the States, 'I'm sorry but my first priority is to be with Chris and I still think I can adjust even in the shorter period of time.' Against a background of their growing love for each other, he found many of the things he valued were shifting in importance.

When he finally turned up for the pre-match training he found himself under a great deal of pressure not to let the side down. 'There was a bit of an atmosphere in the dressing-room because the guys thought I should have been there earlier,' he recalled.

John's form in practice did nothing to calm his nerves and raise his level of confidence – he could hardly hit a ball in the court. His father remembers having a fraught lunch with him the day of his singles rubber against John Alexander when he was panicking, too nervous to eat more than a mouthful of fish.

Buster Mottram had beaten Tony Roche in the opening singles and if John won against Alexander, Britain would be well on the way with a 2–0 lead to a place in the finals for the first time in forty-one years. But John Barrett was worried, as were many others, given John's state: 'We all feared the worst,' he remembered.

When the match began, sure enough things went badly. John lost his first serve to love, Alexander's to love and was 0–30 down: he had lost ten points in a row.

'I was out there thinking this could be the worst defeat in history; I was getting annihilated,' John remembered, his level of desperation rising as he served again and managed to win his first point.

'The whole crowd stood up and roared as if he'd won the match,' Mr Lloyd remembered, which is precisely what John proceeded to do with a display of quite outstanding tennis from that thoroughly unpromising start. He swept John Alexander aside 7–5, 6–2, 6–2, feeling as though the ball was simply gliding off the strings of his racket.

'It was like playing with a football; the ball was so big that wherever it came to I could just hit a winner off it.'

John Barrett saw it unquestionably as John's best match: 'It was one of those fine weather days when his tennis flowed and you could see the confidence in him as he started to win;' and Rex Bellamy in *The Times* wrote, 'Lloyd was affected by an approximation of genius which is akin to madness.'

Mrs Lloyd remembers an Australian commentator exaggerating, 'The way John Lloyd played today he could have beaten God.'

Unfortunately, the win turned out to be a flash in the pan for only a month later in November at the London Benson and Hedges tournament (where the previous year he'd been a finalist against Borg) John lost to Stan Smith, the intense US player, in the opening round. This was the start of a nightmare run of defeats for John which would stretch into the following spring.

John and Chris met up again in early December when she joined him at the sumptuous Mission Hills Country Club in Palm Springs, California where John and his brother David were in the Davis Cup team playing the United States in the final. The American team included John McEnroe for the first time and he soundly defeated John in the singles, helping his side achieve a resounding 4–1 victory.

John and Chris soon forgot the disappointment of John's defeat because they were so wrapped up in their love for each other. They had dinner one evening with fellow-player Ray Moore and his wife Rose at their home in Rancho Mirage, an exclusive resort outside Palm Springs thickly peppered with ex-presidents, celebrities, film stars, multi-millionaires and swish golf and tennis clubs the size of Monaco on wide urban highways with names like Bob Hope, Frank Sinatra and Gerald R. Ford Drives.

The privacy and climate of Palm Springs, a desert paradise 120 miles east of Los Angeles, captivated the Lloyds, as did the Moore's small but attractive house which John and Chris now own. They make it their winter retreat for some weeks each year and escape there for a few days whenever they are in Los Angeles.

'It's worth it even for a few days – that's all you need to recharge your batteries,' said Chris.

It is a single-storey, three-bedroom, two-bathroom vacation home in a country club complex. It's homely and informal with an open plan living area, including a dining space, where visitors are likely to fall over racket bags and other tennis paraphernalia littered about the place.

There's little to identify it as the house of a tennis champion apart from a framed colour cover of *People* magazine featuring Chris and John and one or two other publicity shots on the walls, but they're far outnumbered by Chris's favourite family photos. Some of the crystal she has won sits on the glass coffee table and there's an 'I Love Tennis'-ball magnet affixed to the fridge door in the small kitchen. In a house which they use relatively little the Lloyds have created a loved and lived-in feeling and a very welcoming atmosphere.

An artificial palm tree stands in one corner and on the bookshelves in the other John's video tapes outnumber the paperbacks. Outside is one of the greens of the club's golf course and across the road a communal swimming pool and whirlpool which they share with the neighbouring houses.

The spectacular views of the surrounding mountains, the beautiful sunsets and, even in winter, the sunshine, make it an ideal haven.

John and Chris told Mr and Mrs Lloyd of the engagement when they had come to Palm Springs to watch David and John compete in the Davis Cup final, but John hadn't yet met Mr Evert and was very apprehensive.

'I'd heard lots of stories about him. Chris had told me that he was very straight, very strict and very conservative and I didn't know what to expect. Besides, an airport isn't exactly the greatest place to meet your future father-in-law.'

They were finally introduced by Chris a few days later in the first class JAL lounge at Los Angeles airport as she and her father departed for Tokyo in mid-December where she was competing in a tournament. Quaking though he was, John made quite a favourable impact on Mr Evert. 'My first impression of him then was just like it is now. I'd heard all sorts of good things about him and he certainly is an attractive young man. Chrissie seemed happy so I was pleased about it all.'

Later in December, with their tennis commitments for the year completed, John and Chris met up again at the Evert's Fort Lauderdale home where their engagement was due to be officially announced on 21 December, Chris's twenty-fourth birthday.

Shopping for an engagement ring was one priority before the engagement announcement. 'I wanted a pear-shaped diamond but we couldn't find one so we bought a marquis,' Chris recalled. She proudly showed the ring off to her mother.

'Before you start wearing it don't you think John should have a talk with your father?' Mrs Evert asked, with an eye to the traditional way of doing things. 'I'm proper,' Mrs Evert admitted when asked why she adhered to this slightly old-fashioned protocol. 'I think it's good for the young man and it's nice for the relationship between him and his father-in-law afterwards.'

Chris's first fiancée, Jimmy Connors, had once stewed outside

Mr Evert's Holiday Park office five years before, summoning up the courage to go in and ask for Chris's hand in marriage, and John procrastinated just as furiously about getting this over with.

This somewhat irritated his future wife. 'I got a little annoyed at times. John is a real last minute guy and I'm a bit that way too. Sometimes faults in other people annoy you more when you know they're your faults as well.'

Every day Chris enquired, 'Have you talked to him yet?' to be answered with John's regular excuse, 'No, it isn't the right time.'

With the official announcement imminent, it was Mr Evert who finally sought out John for their talk when the latter was watching *Mission Impossible* on the television with Chris's eleven-year-old sister Clare who had become an instant fan of her eldest sister's good-looking boyfriend. John recalls, 'Mr Evert stood in the doorway and asked, "Good programme, John?" and I said, "Really good scene." He went on, "I think we should have a chat now," so we went into another room.'

Clare stifled her giggles as John got up off the sofa because she knew this was 'the talk'.

'Mr Evert said, "I've heard that it's serious between you and Chris and that you're thinking of getting married, aren't you?" I said, "Yes, I was going to come and tell you that we were getting engaged." He said, "That's very nice and I hope you'll be very happy," and we shook hands. I didn't say a word really, but I thought what a brave person I'd been. Chris came back and I said, "I did it."'

Mr Evert chuckled when asked why Chris's boyfriends were so terrified of him and he sympathized with their having to make the formal approach to their future father-in-law. 'It's not an easy thing to do,' he said, remembering his own experience with Colette's father when he went to ask if he could marry her. 'There's always the possibility that he might start quizzing you about certain things. I think Colette's father was a little tougher on me than I was on Jimmy or John because he didn't know me quite as well and he wanted to be sure Colette was taken care of.'

He remembered his talk with John wasn't nearly such a comprehensive one. 'It wasn't very lengthy because they had already decided that they were going to get married. It was the kind of formality which perhaps I wouldn't have insisted upon although Colette did. I didn't want to make a big thing out of it.'

Chris was well aware that John would be laying himself open to all manner of comments for marrying a tennis star whose fortune was estimated at several million dollars. 'I had often thought that it would be very difficult for someone to marry me unless they were as famous or more famous than me. There's both the money side of my fame, and the success I've made of my career which would be very hard for some people to live with. John is a quality guy with a lot of dignity and class but he doesn't have a big ego, and I saw that he wouldn't feel at all threatened either by my money or my fame. John was a schoolgirls' idol over in England so whenever anyone saw us it was never, "There's Chris, and who is she with?", it was, "Oh, there are Chris Evert and John Lloyd." That's not a reason for marrying someone, but it did make things easier and put John in a less awkward position.'

For his part, John fleetingly considered what life was going to be like for him married to a tennis legend whose success he couldn't hope to emulate, whose earnings were superior to his by several noughts and whose fame and personality would inevitably put him in the shade, but he was disinclined to dwell on the problems.

'I was madly in love and nothing else really entered my mind,' he remembered.

Certainly John didn't think too long or hard about the realities not only of marrying Chris the girl, but also of taking on a quasi-public role as the husband of a celebrity. Nor did he realize the consequences – that in future his every achievement on the court, however commendable in its own right, would be undermined because in comparison to his wife's 'great-of-greats' record it could only pale.

John and Chris decided on 17 April – four months ahead – as their wedding day because it wouldn't interfere with their spring tournament commitments but would enable them to have a leisurely honeymoon and leave adequate practice time for the European circuit and Wimbledon in June.

Chris, with her close family and staunch Catholic background, naturally opted for a traditional white wedding and she worked with her mother on the arrangements: 'She gave me a list of the people she wanted to invite. It was to be a small wedding – we both agreed on that,' Mrs Evert said.

In due course invitations were sent out just to relatives and close friends: 'Mr and Mrs James Andrew Evert request the honour of your presence at the marriage of their daughter Christine Marie . . .'

Chris threw herself wholeheartedly into a bride's routine of wedding preparations and bought books and magazines for ideas for her own and her bridesmaids' dresses. She had already asked Ted Tinling to make her wedding dress – an order which was one of the most unusual and cherished he has ever received.

Earlier that autumn Chris had asked him to run her up some dresses in which to play Federation Cup, the Australian women's international team championship which was started in 1963 to mark the fiftieth anniversary of the International Tennis Federation in Australia.

Ted had made four very fetching halter-neck tennis dresses in record time. But then in Melbourne shortly before Chris was to play, he discovered that she never wore a bra with halter-necks yet he hadn't lined the dresses so they would have been see-through. In his hotel bedroom Ted frantically resorted to do-it-yourself – not a problem since he is an expert with a needle and always carries a sewing kit – using for linings the Christian Dior handkerchiefs his staff had given him as a good luck present before he left for Melbourne.

'It wasn't any fun at all lining four very curvaceous bodices in such a short time,' he remembered, and to get his own back he sewed the very ornate 'T' on the last handkerchief prominently on to the bust of the fourth dress.

The American team won the Cup by a hair's breadth and at the celebration dinner Ted sent the half handkerchief he had left over across to Chris for her autograph. 'Thank you for the lovely dresses,' she wrote, and added, 'Don't forget you still owe me the most important one of all.' He guessed straight away that she meant a wedding dress.

By the time it came to making the actual gown Chris had definite ideas about what she wanted. 'Ted had a few sketches of the latest Paris fashion wedding gowns but I felt they were a little too modern for me. One was a mini, another was a mini with pants; Ted wanted to be different.' Chris told him exactly what she wanted: she loved lace and knew from countless tennis dresses that the style which suited her best was a scooped neck and fitted waist. 'Ted made a beautiful dress which fitted like a dream,' she said, thrilled with the finished effect.

The £3,000 dress was made of white satin and chantilly lace, embroidered with 2,000 pearls and complete with a dramatic ten-foot train.

The closer her wedding day drew, the more tennis took a back seat for Chris. She honoured her tournament commitments but her heart wasn't in the game. 'I was distracted by getting married. I was only practising an hour a day instead of three, and was more interested in choosing the china and the silver.' For the first time in years, the home-loving girl in her was quite naturally asserting itself.

In March, a month before her marriage, Chris lost three times in seven days, all in the £150,000 Avon Championships in the United States – to Sue Barker in Boston, 6–3, 6–1; to Tracy Austin, 6–3, 6–1 and to the Australian left-hander, Dianne Fromholtz, 6–3. 6–3, both in New York. It was the first time since she was seventeen that she had lost more than once in a row.

The headlines in the sports pages gave Chris a hard time: 'Ice maiden turns to slush,' blazed one. 'They were quick with the knocks and the sarcasm,' Chris recalled, and after the Fromholtz defeat she couldn't face the compulsory press conference.

'I felt that getting married was the biggest step of my life and that the media wasn't being very sympathetic. I was prepared to pay the fine but didn't want to go in to talk to the press.' Instead she issued a statement saying that she had searched for her competitive fires during the match but they weren't there. She promised to be back with her characteristic eagerness in the summer.

John's tennis was in the same state as Chris's; he hadn't won a match all winter. However, his wife-to-be had set him another objective – passing his driving test.

John had never had any inclination to drive. He preferred, somewhat extravagantly, to use taxis and hire-car services. In the suburbs of Fort Lauderdale, where there is a dearth of public transport, Chris quickly tired of having to take him around. 'I drove him everywhere; pretty soon I was thinking of going out and buying myself a chauffeur's cap,' she recalled, wincing at the memory. 'He wanted to go to the video store and I wanted to lie in the sun but he made me take him to the store.'

John didn't offer to learn to make himself mobile. 'He needs to be pushed,' Chris explained and so she issued an ultimatum that she wouldn't marry him until he could drive.

Years before, John Barrett, who had taught David Lloyd to drive, had attempted to give John a few lessons but without success: 'John being a much lazier person altogether never really caught on,' he remembered. 'When you haven't got that confidence and co-ordination it's very frightening driving with someone you know in the same car. And there were several scary moments.'

One experience had been in the Wimbledon car park when John confused the brake and the accelerator and almost ploughed through a fence. It had put both instructor and pupil off totally.

Chris offered to teach John but found, as John Barrett had, that John lacked a motorist's aptitude and this almost resulted in their engagement being broken off. During one of her lessons a block away from the Evert's house, Chris snapped, 'You're too close to the side of the road.' 'All right, that's it,' John fired back. 'I'm never going to drive with you again.' 'He drove right home, he was panicking,' remembered Chris.

John waited until a week before the wedding and then took daily driving lessons. Much to Chris's amusement he would edge out of the drive painfully slowly at seven o'clock each morning in the driving-school car with the sign on top, clutching the wheel nervously. Miraculously he scraped through the test but still hates driving and won't drive on the left-hand side of the road in Britain. Parking is his pet hate.

'I'm the sort of person who, if I see a parking space which looks a little bit small and there are cars behind me, rather than trying to get into it and risk people hooting their horns, which makes me nervous, I'll drive on and park half a mile away and walk back. To this day I'm still what you'd call a very dodgy driver.'

Even the metallic grey BMW, which Chris gave him in 1984, hasn't turned John into a motorist and he uses it strictly for pottering around Palm Springs. Ron Samuels and Kathy Smith still laugh at the memory of John almost causing a riot at a drive-in movie in California when he couldn't park close enough to the sound system.

Learning to drive during the week before his wedding meant that John neglected everything else and woke up on the day needing to buy a decent pair of black shoes, a bow-tie and to make up a speech. Fortunately he had decided against the traditional stag party the night before so felt up to doing some shopping. 'I was paranoid about making a speech and having a hangover would have made it even worse,' he said. Besides, he'd always wanted to be sober enough to enjoy his wedding.

The couple were married by the principal of Chris's old high school, Father Vincent Kelly, in a romantic candlelit ceremony at St Anthony's Church in Fort Lauderdale. There were over one hundred guests – John's family and friends from Southend, tennis players like Rosie Casals and Martina Navratilova. Ilie Nastase and Vitas Gerulaitis were invited but unable to come. Ingrid Bentzer, who had introduced them, was there, and Stephanie Tolleson, who had drawn Chris's attention to John when she was watching him on television, was one of the bridesmaids with Chris's old schoolfriends, Laurie Fleming and Ana Leaird, and her youngest sister Clare. Chris's other sister Jeanne, who had recently married Brahm Dubin, was maid of honour.

David Lloyd was best man and he added to John's nerves because it was touch and go whether he'd make it in time. He had to fly in from Holland where he'd been playing tennis and only arrived a couple of hours before Chris and John walked down the aisle.

The four times US Open winner and twice Wimbledon victor was a more nervous bride than she had even been tennis champion as she left home with her father for the church.

'Firstly, there were about a hundred people outside the house and I was shocked that the public viewed this as a big deal in Fort Lauderdale – it's not as though it was Los Angeles or London. I wondered how they had found out where I lived. Then there were another six hundred people waiting at the entrance to the church.'

Chris and her father had got through the well-wishers outside their house and were on the way to the church when they had to turn round and go back because Chris had forgotten her bouquet.

When she finally arrived at the church she couldn't stop shaking. 'I guess I was terrified because I wasn't in my tennis clothes. I'm used to appearing in front of people in those,' she said, making an analogy with an actress out of costume. 'It wasn't as if I was afraid of actual marriage, but when I walked up the aisle I wasn't thinking the things you're supposed to think such as, "I'm so happy, this is going to be a great marriage." I was hoping I would get up the aisle without fainting. I just wanted to get through the ceremony.'

Just as Mr Evert was about to take Chris's arm to start up the aisle Stephanie Tolleson tripped over and fell flat on her face, a rather clumsy breach of decorum which relaxed both bride and bridesmaids.

There were two emotionally charged moments during the ceremony: the first when Chris at the altar took a yellow rose from her bouquet and walked over and presented it to her mother. 'Sometimes the mother of the bride gets pushed out of the picture because the father gives his daughter away and the bride is the centre of attention. Mom had done all the work and I wanted to thank her,' Chris said.

The second was the rendition on the guitar of 'Sunrise, Sunset' from *Fiddler on the Roof* which reduced Ana Leaird to tears.

Chris's visible trembling calmed John who thought at least he should be strong, but his nerves returned when he realized that he had to repeat his wedding vows into a microphone, which had been specially installed so that the people at the back of the church could hear them. Previously he had thought he would be able to get through by mumbling, happy in the knowledge that no one would be able to hear his mistakes.

At the end the wedding photos were taken at the back of the

church because of the throng of people outside. Peter Risdon, who was one of the ushers, remembers being practically blinded by the battery of television lights and popping flashbulbs when he opened the doors afterwards. From the intimacy of their wedding ceremony John and Chris stepped out as husband and wife into the media melée.

John got through his speech adequately at the reception at a nearby hotel which ended with a round of emotional goodbyes and a happy result for two of John and Chris's wedding guests. A year later, Val Ziegenfuss, who had caught Chris's bouquet, married Dale Bradshaw, who had caught John's garter belt.

The honeymoon in Bermuda was slightly sabotaged by the weather. They had chosen Bermuda because John had been there before and remembered blissful hours of lying in the sun. What he hadn't done was check the temperatures in April.

'Our honeymoon was a kind of disaster; well, not a disaster exactly but it didn't turn out to be really great,' was Chris's verdict.

To begin with, they almost weren't allowed on the island, both having left their passports behind because they didn't think they would need them. A lot of lighthearted, 'We just got married, don't you know who we are?' and production of driving licences (in John's case brand new) solved the problem.

Their fame left the honeymooning couple little privacy. They turned on the television and what should they see but their wedding. They were recognized everywhere, whether in the hotel lobby or huddling together on the beach when the temperature unobligingly refused to climb even as high as 70 degrees fahrenheit and the weather remained cloudy and blustery.

They decided on an abrupt change of plan when Chris called home and casually enquired about the weather. 'About 85 degrees and sunny,' came the news. 'We could do with some sun,' declared John; 'I'll make the reservations' – not the first time a honeymoon couple have gone home early.

'We came back and spent a few days in Fort Lauderdale at home and that's when we had a great time. It was hot and we went to the beach every day,' remembered Chris, and the honeymoon was redeemed.

'That was a compliment to us too,' laughed Mrs Evert.

Both Lloyds found getting geared up for tennis after their honeymoon much harder than they had imagined. Chris particularly found a great deal of contentment just in the feeling of being 'settled'. 'If I was losing matches I told myself that it was too much of an effort to be hungry enough to win. I wasn't too upset about it. I found to my surprise that I was into cooking for, and pleasing, John – looking nice for him and sharing tournament responsibilities.'

Tennis practice more often than not consisted of a relaxed session between spouses rather than a serious constructive workout and it soon showed.

Chris's first match after their honeymoon was the Federation Cup in Madrid where she had to struggle to beat Dianne Fromholtz in three sets, 2–6, 6–2, 8–6. More importantly, practising with Tracy Austin she realized just how hungry and how capable the young player was of taking points and games off her. It served as a warning to Chris of how much Tracy had improved and the growing threat she posed.

John was still on honeymoon as far as his game was concerned, and he blamed his lack of motivation on having just got married. 'I just didn't want to even see a tennis ball,' he remembered. His run of defeats mounted before it ended at the French Open in June.

That summer the newlyweds' eyes were really opened to the strains of trying to run two tennis careers in one household when they both suffered emotionally draining and dramatic defeats. It started at the Italian Open in Rome in May. Chris had won her first major international title at the Italian Open in 1974 when she beat Martina Navratilova 6–3, 6–3, and she was usually happy playing on her favourite surface of slow European clay. John, however, had never felt comfortable at the Foro Italico whether playing in the Open or Davis Cup because he loathed the noisy volatile Italians. The ballboys were notorious for playing infuriatingly distracting tricks, especially if you dared to beat one of their favourites.

John had overcome all the difficulties the previous year, in 1978, when he reached the quarter-finals before being beaten by American Eddie Dibbs, the no. 4 seed, 6–2, 6–1.

In the 1979 Open, the Lloyds's problems came in the shape of Tracy Austin for Chris and a seemingly insurmountable self-destructive instinct for John which was to recur frequently during the next few years.

Chris was devastated by her defeat by Tracy Austin in the semi-finals. Tracy, in pigtails, braces and pinafore dresses, was one of the crop of ambitious teenagers Chris's own example as a young prodigy had inspired.

What galled Chris was that Tracy was a carbon copy of herself but younger and better. She rated her as the Jimmy Connors of women's tennis. 'I knew that unless I was hungry Tracy would be hard to beat, because she did everything better than me. I was known for my groundstrokes and along came this little girl who had better groundstrokes. It was the first time someone matched me. She moved better, she hit the ball harder and it was frustrating to have someone eight years younger doing all that to me. She was so young that she could only improve.'

In the semi-finals Tracy won the first set 6–4 and Chris the second 6–2. A tense tie-breaker in the third set was the decider and Chris attributed her opponent's victory to the fact that she was more aggressive and took more chances.

'I remember that I got her up to the net and hit a tipping lob over her head, but she jumped up and nailed it,' Chris said. Tracy took that point and subsequently the tie-breaker 7–4.

'I played not to lose, but she played to win,' Chris concluded.

The wounding defeat also ended Chris's 125-match clay court winning streak which had begun in 1973 at the US Clay Court Championships. This was a tribute to her supremacy on clay which had been 'her surface' since she had started the game and a record of which she was justifiably proud.

After the final and back at her hotel, alone because John was playing a tournament elsewhere and not due to arrive for a couple of days, Chris took her defeat hard. 'I was crying because I thought an era had ended. What a way to go – 7–6 in the third set. If it had been love–love in two sets the win would have been more decisive.'

It was a particular blow that she hadn't been able to find that champion's ingredient which had been her hallmark – coming through and winning when she'd been in a tight corner. 'I thought, I win most close matches so why couldn't I have a little luck this time?'

John flew in to Rome unexpectedly and went straight to the Holiday Inn, where players stay because it has two clay courts to practise on. The first people he saw in the lobby were Evonne and Roger Cawley and he asked them how Chris had got on, expecting to hear news of a win. When he met Chris in their room he found it hard to console her because he hadn't seen the match and couldn't comment.

Chris was heartened and touched that he'd come and they stayed up until four in the morning. The next day, however, bleakness and depression overwhelmed her as she realized that marriage and top tennis looked like being a tough combination.

Worse was to follow when John too suffered a defeat in the men's Italian Championships, which were played the fortnight after the women's. He played Phil Dent, a highly ranked Australian player and former semi-finalist, in the opening round, with Chris watching from the terracing beside the end-court in the warm Italian sunshine. John Barrett arrived just after the match had started and sat down next to Chris.

'How is it going?' he enquired.

'Really well. I'm so pleased to see him playing this way,' she replied, feeling proud as Phil Dent tried unsuccessfully to beat John from the net and John retaliated with some accurate passing shots.

John had established a secure lead of 6–2 in the first set and was 3–0 up in the second when the turnaround inexplicably happened. John Barrett recalled, 'Suddenly Dent came in and John went for a passing shot down the line which was a good shot but out by three or four inches. You could see his whole attitude change; his head hung low, he shrugged and berated himself. You could hear him muttering, "Oh, it's no good, I can't play," and from that moment on he decided that he was going to lose. He programmed himself to lose.' John did not win another game in the match and lost 6–2, 3–6, 0–6.

For Chris it was agonising to watch and her astonishment turned first to despair, as John seemed to make no attempt to recover the initiative, then to quiet anger.

'I was absolutely devastated. In my mind he just didn't try. I had given up a tournament in Berlin to fly in and watch him – the only other player I'd ever done that for was Jimmy Connors and he'd bust a gut on court, fought for every point. I knew I could only take a couple of these weak displays and I said to him afterwards, "I don't care if you lose every match, but why do you humiliate yourself out there? You've got no guts. It doesn't matter what you do – paint walls if you like – but put your heart into it." I felt he was taking things out on me because he couldn't cope with the pressure of being married to no. 1 in the world.'

John found it hard to explain then and still does now. But with astonishing frankness, he does admit: 'I was willing myself to lose, not to win. My career has been a cop-out a lot of the time; it's been taking the easy way out. It sounds so stupid; it sounds like you're an alcoholic.'

It was another disastrous Lloyd defeat in little over a month of married life.

Chris, who is seldom down for long, rebounded and beat Caroline Stoll on clay in a tournament in Vienna. This started her on a second clay-court winning streak which would reach sixty-four successes in a row before Hana Mandlikova ended it in the semi-finals of the French Open in 1981.

In Paris, in June 1979, Chris had an easy win over Wendy Turnbull 6–2, 6–0 to regain her French Open title for the first time since 1975 and have her confidence boosted for Wimbledon which was only weeks away.

John couldn't follow suit so spectacularly but he did beat the French player, Bernard Fritz, 6–3, 3–6, 6–2, 6–7, 6–3 in the same tournament, watched by both Chris and the British Davis Cup captain, Paul Hutchins.

It wasn't a great victory but it was at least a win which John sorely needed as he was beginning to feel that he was doomed to be a permanent loser. However, his recovery was only temporary and in the second round he lost to another Frenchman, Dominique Bedel.

The defeats continued with another at Surbiton just before Wimbledon when Australian Kim Warwick beat him in a match in which John could only ruefully blame himself for inconsistent play and too many double faults. What worried him more than the individual defeats was his general lack of motivation. As he said at the time, 'Normally with Wimbledon coming up I am motivated but this year I'm not looking forward to it. I can't win a match and I don't think I am ever going to win one again. I don't deserve to win when I keep serving double faults in every service game.

Wimbledon provided no respite; John suffered another miserable first-round singles defeat by Swede Ove Bengston, 6–3, 6–4, 6–1, and his downward spiral seemed to be accelerating. This loss was partially mitigated when John and his younger brother Tony had a magnificent doubles win over the second seeds, Tom Okker and Wojtek Fibak. It was a thrilling match and Court One was packed even though the last set was played at eight o'clock in the evening. John and Tony subsequently lost to Australians Phil Dent and John Alexander in the third round, but the earlier win had temporarily raised John's morale.

It was Chris – in her first Wimbledon as Mrs J. M. Lloyd which earned her a warmer reception from the crowds – who was crestfallen after her defeat by Martina Navratilova in the final for the second year running. The score was 6–4, 6–4 and it was all over in an hour as Martina played tennis with supreme energy and skill. Chris's standard was way below her best as Martina served hard and deep, putting away some impressive backhand volleys.

At least after their Wimbledon matches Chris and John could go home instead of back to another anonymous hotel room. They were staying in John's small bachelor flat in Wimbledon during the tournament and it enabled them to enjoy a semblance of normal married life for a few weeks. Their rushed courtship of snatched days in hotels followed by the first months of married life on the tennis circuit had meant that they'd missed out on really getting to know each other and had quite a bit of adjusting to do.

From the outset it was clear that theirs was no ordinary marriage: they were either together round the clock or apart, on different continents. It was all or nothing, and Chris described how hard this was to come to terms with: 'When we were together we were glued to each other, then John or I would go away to a tournament and I would really miss him. That's when I had to learn to adjust and really get into my tennis rather than sitting and sulking by the phone each day.'

One of the early differences that emerged between them was their getting-up times. Chris, unlike John, is not a morning person. 'I like to sleep until at least nine o'clock. When I was single I used to wake up around eleven o'clock in the morning but since I've been married I've come down to around nine o'clock which I think is quite good. John usually gets up at about eight.'

John found his life-style on the tennis circuit considerably upgraded by the acquisition of a wealthy wife and from staying with other guys in a single motel room and going to the launderette he found himself in luxury suites using the hotel laundry service.

'John came up to my financial level but he never took advantage of the position like so many husbands of famous wives do. I don't think I could have married a man who took it better than John,' Chris said.

John had, in fact, cultivated some expensive tastes before he married and he introduced Chris to caviare on a Concorde flight. Normally, however, their diet was less exotic although they did have different tastes in food. John, from childhood, had had a sweet tooth and adores traditional English desserts – treacle tart, suet puddings and hot custard – which Chris started eating when she met him and gained a few pounds in weight.

'John doesn't really go in for chocolate though,' said Chris, 'and I love it, especially chocolate mousse, soufflé and profiteroles. He likes plainer food – he's like his dad in that way. He'll go to a French or Italian restaurant but that's it whereas I'm more adventurous. I love Chinese food and I'll try Japanese and other ethnic varieties.'

Nowadays they have both become more health-conscious about their diets, although they don't fanatically monitor every morsel which goes into their mouths, unlike some players. 'I have dessert sometimes and an occasional glass of wine,' Chris said. 'John is stricter than I am. He has cereal from the health food shop for breakfast with bananas; he never eats butter or sugar and tries to cut out oil. Butter is my luxury but now I'm trying to cut down on it. I like the occasional diet drink, too, which John thinks is terrible because of what's in it. He is really into natural foods and is making me eat more whole-grain breads and pasta. I do think they make you feel better and increase your energy, whereas certain foods seem to take away your energy.'

Both drink only sparingly – John has a beer from time to time and Chris enjoys white wine. In their hotel suites the empties are mineral water rather than champagne bottles, and the top of the television is usually covered in rows of bottles, tins and packets of vitamins, minerals, unsalted nuts, cereals and honey.

Chris thinks of John as a thoroughly undemanding husband. 'He doesn't believe in male and female roles so if I cooked him a meal he saw it as a luxury, a real treat.' However, marriage did inspire her to learn some recipes. 'I enjoyed cooking for John and I suppose too that I began to appreciate what my mom had done for five children every night while we were growing up. The dinner was on the table every night, and it was always something different.'

Mrs Evert passed on some of her culinary secrets to Chris and in turn is full of praise for her daughter's efforts in the kitchen: 'She's a great cook and does marvellous things with eggs. I think she'll enjoy it one day, she just hasn't had the time yet.'

Chris is very adept at making her mother's speciality. 'My mother taught my sister and I to cook this great spaghetti sauce which takes about two hours. It's made with lean chopped beef, onion, garlic, herbs, spices and tomato sauce. I usually serve it with a big salad containing about ten different vegetables, and garlic bread. I make that more than anything else when we have company.'

'Colette's spaghetti parties', featuring Mrs Evert's speciality, are extremely popular on the tennis circuit whether thrown informally for a group of players at Hilton Head, South Carolina where they sometimes go to practise or in the Lloyds's Kingston home for the visiting American Wightman Cup team.

Cooking has never become a chore for Chris since she spends most of her time in hotels. During Wimbledon, Jenny Scally, their cook/housekeeper, does the catering in their Kingston home so Chris only has a brief spell in the kitchen each year while they are at their Palm Springs house.

She even had John's welfare at heart when he once spent a few days alone at Palm Springs while she was at a tournament: 'I wrote out three recipes and stuck them to the refrigerator door. I said, "Take chicken out, put in glass bowl, turn oven on to 350 degrees, put chicken in oven and bake for one hour, wash potato and bake for one hour." There were two chicken recipes and one for cooking spaghetti and heating up the de-frosted sauce. Every night when I called I asked him, "Did you make the meal?" and he had. I think he was quite happy with himself because before we were married he couldn't even boil water.' He either ate out or resorted to take-aways – during one World Cup when nothing would have moved him from his TV, he ate pizzas night after night.

John, though, proved to be an absolute expert with one household gadget – the video. Chris had no interest in it whatsoever but John was very keen that she should at least learn how to record programmes so she could tape his favourites when he was away.

'I had to learn or he wouldn't talk to me,' Chris said, so since he'd learnt to drive for her she mastered the video controls for him.

They hadn't been married long when they discovered that their tastes in films couldn't be more different either. One night in Melbourne in December 1984 during the Australian Open the definition of Lloyd togetherness was Chris watching Meryl Streep in *Silkwood* on the hotel's in-house movie system in the bedroom of their suite, while in the sitting-room John enjoyed the blood-chilling video *Razorback*, which he'd hired at the local video rental shop.

Having married an American, one of the reasons John had adapted so quickly to living in the United States was the twenty-four hour television service and the number of video stores open at all hours.

As far as tennis was concerned, he'd always preferred playing in the US Open to Wimbledon, in spite of the fact that it is physically more demanding because of the high temperatures, the draining humidity and the hard courts which give your feet more of a pounding than Wimbledon's grass. At least there he finds none of the 'home-boy home-tournament' pressure.

At Flushing Meadow in September 1979 John received an especially warm welcome from the crowd who took him to their hearts, not only as the new husband of their no. 1 woman player but also because he was a likeable, good looking personality, and he found himself developing into something of a star.

He got through to the third round in the tournament, beating Charlie Pasarell and Australian Paul McNamee, before a stomach upset forced him to default in a match against John McEnroe. Twenty-year-old McEnroe went on to defeat Jimmy Connors in the final and when Tracy Austin overwhelmed Chris to become the US Open's youngest ever winner, it became clear that a new generation of tennis champions had arrived. At twenty-seven and nearly twenty-five respectively Jimmy Connors and Chris suddenly looked like the older generation. It wasn't a comfortable feeling.

A barrage of outstanding shots from Tracy had ended Chris's hopes of winning the US Open for the fifth consecutive time thus creating another record. Tracy had blasted back from 4–3 down in the first set and in convincing style had won the next six games. The final 6–4, 6–3 score was a disaster for Chris. 'I was outclassed. I was ready to play and I had improved but she had nerves of steel and got too many balls back. I was crushed.'

Dignified and gracious in defeat, Chris gave Tracy a congratulatory pat on the head and hid her own heartbreak as she comforted her friends Rosie Casals and Martina Navratilova, who were in tears at the court-side because of Chris's emotional defeat.

World Tennis magazine wrote about the defending champion's downfall: 'It almost seemed pre-ordained that Chris should pass her US Open mantle on to Tracy – the only one as young, as poised, as hungry and as nerveless as the sixteen-year-old Evert was in her 1971 debut at Forest Hills. Chris Evert and Tracy Austin are linked together almost like rings around Saturn by the backcourt styles they play, by the two hands they place on the rackets, by their steadfastness under pressure.'

John hadn't been able to stay in New York and support Chris in the final because of a Davis Cup commitment in Rome. Having caused a stir the previous autumn by turning up late he couldn't do it again. He heard the commentary of the match against Tracy from the BBC's Gerald Williams. It made gloomy listening and he felt dreadful that he was away when his wife needed him. As a result they agreed that in future they would always be together during the four Grand Slam events a year.

'It wasn't right for Chris for me to be away in Italy; it was a wrong decision for me to have gone. And as far as my own game is concerned I would have been much better psychologically being with Chris – even though she lost – than spending those extra days practising on Italian clay.'

In fact, John lost both his Davis Cup singles matches and Buster Mottram, who was staying in the next room to John at Rome's Cavalieri Hilton, remembers that the transatlantic phone calls to Chris at two and three o'clock each morning did nothing to help his game.

Alone in her New York hotel room, Chris brooded on her match and the sniping rivalry which was developing between her and Tracy Austin. 'Tracy never gave me a lot of compliments. If someone asked her, "Who did you pattern your game after?" she would dodge the answer. I would think, "You're the mirror image of me – two-handed backhand, court demeanour and everything – so why don't you just admit it?" Mind you, I went out of my way, too, not to give her a lot of credit because I felt threatened by this little girl who could do everything better than me. We were cordial to each other but we weren't friends.'

Chris accompanied John to the Benson and Hedges tournament at Wembley in November where she watched him lose to John McEnroe in fifty-five minutes, 6–4, 6–1. This match confirmed what she already knew – that John was his unhappiest when he was on court.

The tennis year over, the Lloyds went back to Fort Lauderdale for the traditional Evert family Christmas reunion, even larger in 1979 because three of the Evert children – Drew, Chris and Jeanne – had got married that year.

'My father loves to decorate the tree and my mom buys the presents,' said Chris. 'We all give each other gifts. I'm the fortunate one in a way because while everyone else has played tennis I'm the one who actually made it. I love going out and buying gifts; it's my excuse for spending money. I'd rather buy a diamond bracelet for my sister than receive one.'

However, Chris still thought it was a disappointment that now she was married she and John only got one present from the whole family, and rubbed it into her mother. Their gift was another place setting for the silver service her parents had given them for a wedding present.

The Christmas routine has not varied in years – a large turkey dinner on Christmas Eve and ham for lunch on Christmas Day after church. The Everts are staunch Catholics and Chris even dragged a reluctant John along.

'I've never been a big fan of churches; I get very claustrophobic in them,' John admitted. 'I also feel a bit hypocritical going there once a year. The family were pleased that I went but I didn't enjoy it and was looking at my watch the whole time longing to get out.' He loved Christmas in the sun, though: 'I'd rather be in a hot place where I can take my shirt off than sitting in front of a coal fire.'

A tennis family doesn't have a day off on Christmas Day and they all trooped off to the courts at Holiday Park for an hour or so. 'It was like a rest day,' joked Chris.

Fittingly, it was a happy family gathering on which to end the year for a couple who had taken well to married life. 'I felt John and I were kindred spirits, very compatible and the best of friends. Our personalities complemented one another,' Chris said. Nine months of marriage had opened her eyes to the importance of people, relationships and feelings after so many years of thinking only tennis. 'I saw there was more to life than trophies, money and titles,' she said, and enjoyed the discovery.

Looking towards 1980 both Chris and John had a lot of professional and personal priorities to sort out, but celebrating

Christmas and New Year in sun-drenched southern Florida with relations and friends they were self-indulgently in love with each other. And, for the moment, they forgot about tennis.

CHAPTER SIX

1980
Tennis Crises
and Chris's Comeback

'Love Doubles' was a promoter's dream: take the best woman tennis player in the world, Chris Lloyd, partnered by handsome husband, John, playing against the men's no. 1, Bjorn Borg, and his Romanian fiancée, Mariana Simionescu, in a mixed doubles exhibition match.

Add the sort of glamour usually reserved for film premières and other galas; royalty, represented by Princess Anne (whose charities the match was in aid of); linesmen in dinner jackets; a sumptuous champagne buffet; and the resulting evening was bound to be a glittering smash hit.

Exhibition matches – nicknamed 'exos' by the players – are genuine contests played for a big purse: in this case, £40,000 for the victors and £25,000 for the losers – but the results don't affect any of the players' computer rankings.

'Our agents, IMG, who also handled Bjorn, drummed it up and it seemed like a good idea,' Chris remembered. It was promoted with plenty of hype and the £25-tickets were sold out.

The match was relayed live on television to the United States: ABC, the major American network, bought it as a sports exclusive and introduced it to the strains of the song 'Love, Love, Love' with cupids and hearts figuring prominently in the graphics, though the actual venue was a little more humble – a specially erected Big Top tent in London's Battersea Park.

The fifty-eight minute match, which John and Chris won 6–4, 6–3, was played in a relatively unpressurized atmosphere; but nevertheless Chris's furrowed brow beneath her blonde fringe proved that her concentration level was at its usual intense pitch.

It was the first time that John and Chris had played together and he was generous with his praise after the match: 'Chrissie was the best player on the court; she really dominated the exchanges and didn't let Bjorn and Mariana in.'

'He's flattering me,' quipped Chris, holding a bunch of flowers which matched the Hawaiian floral decoration hanging around John's neck, but she admitted that her forte had been to get more first serves in. 'We obviously had to hit to Mariana since Borg is the best player in the world.'

The slightly perfunctory handshakes at the net indicated that the Lloyds and their opponents were acquaintances rather than friends, but the warm applause indicated the audience's appreciation of this famous four's match.

The £40,000 prize money wasn't a lot for Chris who had just won the Italian Open, but partnering his wife was lucrative for John who was not reaping much from his run of early round defeats.

Few of the people in the 3,000 strong crowd could have guessed that both the blonde, tanned Lloyds, who had celebrated their first wedding anniversary a month before and looked so much in love, had in the preceding few months come perilously close to hanging up their tennis shoes and quitting the game for good.

Their doubts about their futures as tennis players had different roots: Chris had slogged so hard, won so many matches and totally dominated women's tennis in the seventies. She had achieved so much that she queried whether she wanted to go on with the incessant grind just to put the icing on the cake. John, on the other hand, had never made a hundred per cent effort to realize his potential and fulfil the promise he'd shown when playing at his best. He'd allowed his form not merely to go off but to sink so drastically that he now had to decide whether he was going to go all out and see if he could resurrect it in a major way, breaking into the top echelons, or abandon his career altogether. Messing around half-heartedly was not doing him, or his marriage, any good at all.

Chris's crisis – a re-run of the one she had suffered over the winter of 1977–8 when she took three months off from the circuit – occurred in February 1980 when, overplayed, overtired and stale she felt she just couldn't keep on relentlessly playing the game at its highest level.

The straw which broke her back was an uncharacteristic spate of defeats at the beginning of 1980. In the Colgate Series – a succession of tournaments in the United States sponsored by Colgate – she lost twice in Washington DC in January to Tracy Austin in the same week, and later in the month she lost again in an Avon Championship tournament in Cincinnati.

She felt that she was at rock bottom, called John and said: 'I have to have you here because I think I'm going to have a breakdown.'

John flew in straight away, and Chris poured out her troubles over a 'crisis' lunch with him, Mrs Evert and Ana Leaird. 'I'm going to pull out,' she told them. 'I know in my heart I have to stop playing. I'm crying every day, I'm unhappy on court and I need to take a break.' It wasn't a question of quitting because she was no longer no. 1; it was a matter of no longer being happy playing the game.

John was shaken by the intensity of the situation. 'She was very emotional and felt frightened to play. She had just had enough,' he said.

It took another bad defeat by Martina Navratilova in Chicago later in January to bring her closer to the brink. Ingrid Bentzer drove John and Chris from the tournament to their hotel on a depressing, freezing cold night as John tried to console his wife in the back of the car.

'You played really well; you only lost by a couple of points,' he said. Chris, in tears, choked out what was really the problem: 'I don't care if I win or lose; I care about doing my best. I couldn't produce my best, that's the whole point,' she said, absolutely stricken at finding her inner resources exhausted.

In Seattle at the end of February she decided she couldn't carry on a moment longer, defaulted in a match against Virginia Wade and elected to pay a $2,000 fine per tournament for pulling out of the next three to enable her to take a break of two months from the game.

'She has just been following the same routine since she was fifteen, and now she needs time to recharge her batteries, focus or re-focus on her goals,' John rationalized as the press blazed, 'Mrs Lloyd burned out.'

Chris agreed that she had reached saturation point: 'I felt I had put my whole life into my tennis. Yet my tunnel vision wasn't as concentrated as in previous years because I had got married and had a husband and a home. I also knew that every year the tennis circuit was getting tougher and tougher. In previous years when I was winning easily I was exerting less mental and emotional energy because often I didn't have a really tough match until the semi-finals. Now I was having taxing matches in the early rounds too because the standard of tennis was higher and the game had more depth.'

Ironically Chris could only blame herself for the higher standard of competition and increase in the number of tournaments; it was her shining example which had helped to accelerate the boom in women's tennis. 'There are a million girls in America who play tennis because of Chris,' Ted Tinling said.

'Evonne Cawley and I encouraged the wave of kids who were starting to play tennis earlier. We showed that the life of a pro-fessional player was appealing – you could travel all over the world, meet people and earn a lot of money. 'Because of television, women's tennis was becoming more visible, and girls saw you didn't have to look like a masculine freak to become an athlete. That encouraged the younger ones.'

Chris courageously decided to take a sabbatical and set a prece-dent in the game for doing this. Since then, long holidays from the circuit have been considered the norm but at the time Chris came in for a lot of censure. Her critics claimed that she had a duty to support the tournaments and that if she pulled out so might the sponsors since was a star player.

'It annoys me that I was criticized for taking a break. A lot of the girls on the tour thought that either I was going to retire or I was attempting to dodge the indoor tournaments. Now look what's happened – because so many of the young players have fallen by the wayside tennis organizers are coming up with the brilliant idea of making the tennis circuit last for only ten months of the year. Yet five years ago I told them it's just not physically possible to play for twelve months of the year and have a long career.'

Pam Shriver was one player who was particularly critical of Chris in 1980 but at the Australian Open four years later publicly boasted how she could hardly wait for the tournament to end so she could start her three months' holiday because she was overtired. Such had the climate changed as a result of Chris's initial move, which was made with great foresight.

Once Chris had extricated herself from the spring tournaments and announced her rest she and John took off for their Palm Springs home for a complete holiday and some profound thinking about the future.

In their cosy three-bedroomed bungalow away from the continual pressure of life on the circuit, with the sun shining brilliantly out of the clear blue desert sky and with a breathtaking glimpse of the mountains from the kitchen window, John and Chris had their first complete break in nine months of married life. They had the opportunity just to enjoy being with each other in a relaxed atmosphere. Gone were the restrictions of life in a first class hotel in the public eye. In Palm Springs Chris had the freedom and privacy to jump out of her car after a practice session at the courts, clad in shorts and top, milkshake and cardboard carton of takeaway sandwiches in one hand, and dash in through the garage door to slump on the sofa and enjoy her snack lunch. For once there was no one's image of Chris Evert, tennis star, to live up to.

Chris is more comfortable now with her celebrity status but she admitted that she has found it awkward in the past. 'I know that people are looking at me because I'm a tennis player. They're not admiring me because I'm a great or a beautiful person, but because I've done one thing brilliantly in my life. I've felt very self-conscious about this. Sometimes I've just wanted to come home and be normal and go out in cut-off shorts and a T-shirt. But if you're an idol you know that people are looking you over from top to toe and discussing your appearance. I still wear sunglasses all the time when I go out.'

Friends who saw Chris and John during those weeks remember too the great romance they were having and the chemistry between them. In a cover story in *People* magazine just after her rest had started, Chris enthused about the pleasures of married life: 'My priorities are different now. My marriage is more important than tennis.'

Chris has very fond memories of her feelings of release: 'It was a tremendous relief just to get up in the morning, make a cup of coffee and sit in front of the TV. I hadn't been able to do that for so long because even when I'd had a week off I knew that I had to practise for the next tournament. I felt as if a weight had been lifted off my shoulders. I remember catching up on my TV soap operas – I've always been a great fan of *General Hospital* and have followed Luke and Laura's love story for ages – and telephone calls to my girlfriends, spending a little more time with my family, and being by myself a bit, figuring out what I wanted to do with my life.'

Although she doesn't like to think that she is easily influenced by other people, Chris values sounding out other people's opinions before making a decision, and she asked her friend Ron Samuels whether he thought she should return to tennis or retire.

He felt strongly that if Chris quit she would later regret it and remembers tendering his advice: 'We were sitting out in the back-yard talking and she said: "I feel I'm getting older and slowing down and it's getting tougher to beat the young kids who are coming up. I don't know how to keep working that hard." I told her, "Whatever you may have lost in speed you've got in experience. You have a mental toughness which none of these other girls has. When they walk out on court and look across the net and see they're playing you it's very intimidating for them."'

As well as a rest, Chris needed some encouragement that she was still the best player in the world and reinforcement of what she basically knew herself – that she could win again. John was immensely supportive and counselled that she should only play if she wanted to, but that if she did she could be no. 1 again. 'I think she had doubts about that,' he remembers.

He had an inkling that this time off would only be an intermission in Chris's career and not the end. 'There were still some aims Chris hadn't satisfied, some goals she hadn't attained.'

Chris, too, knew she couldn't do nothing for long. Even at the height of the crisis in Cincinnati, strained and miserable, she had asked her mother and Ana, 'What kind of things can I do? Because I don't want to just sit around the house all day.'

Between them the parties at that crisis lunch had come up with the obvious suggestion of television commentating, and, as it turned out, viewing the game from the commentary box helped re-kindle Chris's appetite for tennis.

She covered two tournaments with NBC's commentator, Bud Collins; the first was the final of the Avon Championships at Madison Square Garden, New York, in March, where Tracy Austin beat Martina Navratilova 6–2, 2–6, 6–2.

Ana Leaird remembers that Chris was nervous about how her fans would react to her being in the commentary box because she'd been away from tennis for two months. So Ana suggested to the organizers that they turn a spotlight on Chris to let everyone know she was there. 'By the way, ladies and gentlemen,' the announcement came over the public address system, 'even though she's not on court today we thought you would like to know Chris Lloyd is here up in the TV box. Chris, would you stand up and take a wave?' To her surprise the entire crowd of thirteen thousand people stood up and applauded, with enthusiastic shouts of 'Yeah Chrissie'. Ana said it was as if they wanted to show her that they loved her and that she was still in their hearts although she wasn't playing.

'I got goose-bumps and Chris told me later that she felt a little emotional and hoped that Bud Collins wouldn't ask her a question straightaway because she didn't think she would be able to answer it.'

Chris's debut behind the microphone earned her some flattering compliments from Collins: 'Most newcomers tend to blab too much because they get nervous on TV,' he said. 'For someone doing it for the first time, Chris was way above anyone I've ever worked with. She really was a pro, just as she is in everything else she does.'

Chris commentated on a second tournament at Amelia Island, Florida, in which Martina played Hana Mandlikova, but discovered that however good a player you are, broadcasting concise, informative comments during a match is an exacting business.

'For some reason my mind went blank; I'm much better when people ask me questions. When you're commentating it's not the same because you have to give your opinion about a certain shot. You have to be really smart to commentate well.'

The two tournaments had performed a vital function by rekindling her enthusiasm for a comeback; nevertheless she knew she still wasn't quite ready to step on court again. 'I got excited because I realized that I would prefer to be out there playing again instead of sitting and watching.'

As a child Chris had felt, 'Wind me up and I'll walk on court,' and now she realized almost automatically that it was more natural for her to go back to tennis than to quit.

'Whenever I have taken time off from the circuit to rest I've never really felt that I had to go back because I loved or needed the game so much. It was always my choice to go back because tennis was my career and where my talent lay. It was still comfortable for me to play and I still enjoyed the lifestyle that went with the game, but I learnt that I was going to have to pace myself and not get jaded or burnt out.

'I felt, "OK, you've had your rest and your vacation; now you should be refreshed and willing to go back on the tour." It wasn't, "Oh, I can't wait to play again." But I felt fresher, I enjoyed practising a little more and I was enjoying my matches.'

Chris also knew that the longer she took off the less she would want to start all over again. 'If I took six months or a year off I might not want to come back at all. I knew I still had it in me to play well.'

She was practising well, too, for two or three hours a day at Mission Hills, and hitting with John helped enormously.

'It's great for my game to practise with John because he does everything better than me. He pushes me more than the girls could, and besides, you don't like to practise with the top girl players because you have to compete against them. Of course, it was much better for me than it was for him. He knows my weaknesses and what shots to feed me to improve them. He made me move round the court more nimbly and to play a little more quickly from the baseline to get my opening to come into the net.'

John Barrett was just one observer who was impressed by John's contribution to Chris's success. 'He used to encourage her enormously, both verbally and by practising hard with her. All the time he was trying to sharpen her up and make her move quicker, sharpen her volley and her reflexes. Her court coverage improved dramatically and she became much quicker about the court.'

Contrary to popular belief a match between the two Lloyds would not be a close contest. 'If John and I played I think I could get a game off him but he would beat me very badly,' Chris said, and John added, 'If I unleashed my full power then it would all be over very quickly because a man can simply overpower a woman even though she might be a better player technically.'

'A lot of people have this misconception that the two top women players could compete with the top 50 or top 100 men, but that's wrong; the no. 1 woman in the world would have trouble with the top 1000 men,' Chris said. 'Men are stronger, more powerful and quicker. I was never able to beat either of my brothers when they were college players and I was no. 1 in the world.'

John reckoned that when he's practising with Chris he slows his shots down by five or ten per cent so they get some good rallies. Then when he goes back to play against men, although he may be hitting the ball well he finds himself hitting it a fraction late.

During Chris's break John was working with coach Dennis Ralston in Palm Springs and Chris joined them too for the occasional training session. As a result the Lloyds hired Ralston, who had been captain of the US Davis Cup team and a Wimbledon finalist in the sixties, to travel with them for a while. Chris wanted to work with him not only because he was someone to hit with, but also because he knew the games of the other women players on the circuit so could discuss an opponent's weaknesses with Chris and determine a strategy before a match.

Chris's father had coached her since she was six and probably knows her game better than anyone else, but she felt that as he hadn't travelled with her and kept up to date with the standards of play he wasn't able to advise her how to tackle some of her opponents' newer tactics.

'A couple of times when I went home I found that he thought tennis was the same as it was ten years ago, and he would tell me just to get the ball back and play steadily, instead of encouraging me to play more aggressively.'

Before Chris rejoined the circuit in the spring she travelled with John to support him in his efforts to boost his game but he was unable to retrieve it from a serious, seemingly bottomless, slump. In Washington DC she watched him play South African Bernie Mitton and it was a ghastly experience for both Lloyds. John was humiliated 6–0, 6–0 on court and so was Chris as a spectator off court.

John remembers not even getting into the match – nor really wanting to. 'I froze completely. I wasn't in good shape at all. The ball would come towards me and I felt scared to hit it.'

Chris, sitting with Ingrid Bentzer, was equally uncomfortable – an American in front of an American crowd watching her British husband getting a thrashing.

'It was tough for me to watch John in a tournament because it was America and everyone was looking at me. John was aware of me in the crowd and of people coming up and asking for my autograph. I felt bad for him, not for myself, because I knew how he was feeling about his tennis and being there I put even more pressure on him. John was very good about his losses. He concealed his disappointment whereas I was sulky when I lost. That way John's a lot less moody than I am. I could make the people around me feel uncomfortable when I lost, but he never took his losses out on anyone.'

Unfortunately it wasn't an isolated incident; John regularly lost heart followed closely by losing the game. 'I felt embarrassed to take money for little more than appearing,' he said. 'Really, I don't know why I bothered to play sometimes. I just don't know why I did.'

Things went from bad to worse and, knowing his tennis was dreadful, John found himself often hoping that he could play his match before there was much of an audience so he could get the ordeal over with and make the least spectacle of himself.

It was a long way from the heady times of his heyday – police escorts to get him through his thronging fans at Wimbledon and the wildly applauded dramatic disposal of seeds a lot higher than himself in the rankings. John knew it but adopted a strange detached fatalism about the future. 'I was very concerned in some ways, but then in others I wasn't. I didn't have the strength in me at the time, nor the pull or motivation to get out of it. I just let things slide. I kept telling myself, "There'll always be another day." I thought something would happen, someone would wave a magic wand and I'd suddenly start winning. It was ridiculous.'

Chris needed no fairy godmother to organize her return because she already had it carefully orchestrated herself. She decided that it would be on European clay – the surface on which she had grown up and had had her best results, and away from the pressures of playing in the United States.

As her first tournament she selected the Italian Open in Rome in May, where she beat Hana Mandlikova in three sets to face Romanian Virginia Ruzici in the final. She was finding that it took quite an effort to get back into her stride.

'Playing in a match again was a bit of a foreign feeling to begin with because of my three months off. I wasn't match-tough so I was thinking too much instead of just reacting and being guided by my instincts.'

Although she lost the first set of the final 5–7, she won the next two 6–2, 6–2 – the first tournament win this time round. She followed this in Paris in June with a Grand Slam triumph over Virginia Ruzici 6–0, 6–3 to give her her fourth French crown and confirm that she was back with a vengeance. With the capacity unique to a champion, Chris was back in a winning groove.

'After three or four tournaments I was back on the trail, just instinctively playing again. I was grateful that I hadn't quit for good. I knew I'd made the right decision but I also accepted the fact that there were going to be times when I felt stale and "tennised out" because I had probably practised and played more tennis than anybody else around.'

Her revival gave both Lloyds a positive purpose to concentrate on, but unfortunately although John wholly and constructively supported Chris's comeback he also used it as an excuse to neglect his own game even more.

It's easy to claim, as some of John's fans do, that he sacrificed his career interests in favour of his wife's. But he does not toally agree: 'The truth of the matter is that I didn't want to play. When I went to tournaments I wasn't trying so I spent more time with Chris because basically I was wasting my own time playing how I was playing.'

It was a tribute to Chris's considerable skill that she relaunched her tennis career so successfully, especially when compared to Bjorn Borg, her opponent in that London 'Love Doubles' match. Three years later he took time off then made an abortive return, said farewell to tennis and played his last official tournament in Monte Carlo in March 1983 at the age of twenty-six.

Chris discussed how she had managed it and he hadn't. 'For those five or six years Borg was playing he was the most intense player there has ever been,' Chris said. 'Although I think of myself as disciplined, and having tunnel vision, he was even more so. He practised four hours a day, monitored his food intake and he missed out on a lot. He never took time off, but played twelve months of the year. If he'd wanted a longer career he really should have let up on the exhibitions because he burned himself out. McEnroe, Connors and Lendl were playing so well that I think he figured why be no. 2 or no. 3 after having been no. 1 for so long?'

Since 1980 Chris has had the wisdom to allocate her resources carefully in order to avoid burning herself out permanently, like Borg. 'My first priority is being present at, and thereby supporting, the major tournaments; my second is pacing myself so that I enjoy my rest weeks; my third is exhibitions and special events. I play for a good half of the year; the other half I've got to fulfil my obligations to my endorsements, and then I've also got to be with John.'

Unfortunately, even the Herculean effort she put into her

revival, the professional dedication and determination she showed, didn't rub off on John. At best his attempts at real work were spasmodic. Apart from the occasional erratic spurt he all but abandoned his own game and retreated from its failure by vicariously enjoying his wife's wins rather than trying to emulate her example.

'I looked at it that we were part of a team: when she won, I won and when I won – which wasn't very often – she won.'

Chris remembers feeling frustrated that her motivation didn't inspire John. 'Instead it backfired and worked against him because it was hard for him to live up to my standards.'

The blow of constant losses was cushioned for John because defeat in the early rounds of a tournament – on a Monday or Tuesday – had the hidden bonus that he could hop on a plane and fly to wherever Chris was and spend the rest of the week with her. Doing well meant spending the week apart. This routine quickly became a vicious circle and also did nothing to elevate John's game. By practising with Chris he neglected his own training because playing with a woman was no substitute for a proper workout with a male sparring partner – and it showed. His run of poor performances became more and more prolonged.

In between the French Open in June and Wimbledon in July, their coach, Dennis Ralston, hammered John to a 6–3, 6–3 defeat in the Greater Manchester Gold Shield Tournament at Didsbury and told him bluntly afterwards that he had to learn to 'dig and die for every point'. John had a 4–1 lead when a double fault irked him so much that he switched into his losing syndrome and stopped making any effort, losing the next six games in a row. 'It was distressing to see such a talented player in such a dispirited state,' Ralston said.

The incentive of the approaching Wimbledon tournament awoke John temporarily and he made a sudden burst of effort while working with Dennis Ralston in preparation for it. But it was too little, too late. In the first round he was due to play former adversary Buster Mottram and secretly hoped that the work he had put in might be sufficient to earn him a first round victory then at least he would have started on the road to recovery.

Buster had always freely admitted that he loathed playing on grass, the surface John preferred, so all the conditions seemed to favour a Lloyd victory. But on the day the Lloyd self-doubts took over and Buster remembered that John's sullen mentality was obvious from the warm-up. On court John's hopes of success soon evaporated and Buster fought to win the match as quickly as possible in case the Lloyd of old suddenly asserted himself, but it didn't. John recalled the experience blackly: 'I totally froze up again, and was beaten very comfortably 6–4, 6–2, 6–2.

John Barrett saw the match and thought, 'Buster didn't play particularly well, but John was still self programmed to lose; he was in the middle of his slump.'

Afterwards John felt upset and thoroughly deflated. The defeat underlined the fact that to make a comeback from his low point would require a prolonged spell of work and not just a spurt. 'I had worked hard' – or thought he had – 'but I was looking for an instant reward and they just don't happen after working for only four weeks,' John said. The truth had hit him.

Chris bore the full brunt of his despair: 'That's it, that's my last Wimbledon. I don't ever deserve to play here again,' he told her, close to breaking point. It was a tribute to Chris that this drama didn't distract her from her own game. Instead she dealt with him with the sympathy of a wife and the logic of a highly disciplined player. 'I tried to motivate John by narrowing his choice down, and said, "Let's have a goal for one year: just give the game one hundred per cent for twelve months, then you can quit and hang up your racket."'

For Chris the mental side of the game – concentration and the will to win – came easily, and the physical capabilities needed she had acquired through hard work; to John the physical part came easily, because he relied on his natural ability, but mentally he lacked the necessary determination and competitiveness. Chris partially attributed John's poor performance at Wimbledon against Buster to his procrastination and not being singleminded enough about his match; not sharing her champion's dedicated approach. For example, instead of psyching himself up to go on court before the match, he was dashing round Wimbledon worrying about seats and tickets for his parents and friends.

'I would get angry with him because he'd go out of his way to buy tickets and put them into envelopes an hour before his match, instead of concentrating on preparing to play,' she said. 'That's being a great guy, but as a competitor in the tournament it's not being practical. Since I've met John he has never thought of himself first. He's a totally unselfish man in that respect, and it's a great quality – but it gets in the way of his game.'

Another of John's idiosyncracies which Chris found hard to fathom was his obsession with reading the sports pages the day after a bad defeat, knowing full well that his write-ups would only discourage and depress him. Chris would watch incredulously as John hurried off to the newsagent, returned with a bundle of the national dailies and pored over them.

'Each one would say "Lloyd killed in match", or "Lloyd going downhill", yet he would read them all. I didn't think it helped him one bit. What the journalists said really hurt him and their comments haunted him when he played his next match.

'I remember Dennis Ralston yelling at him, "John, don't read that stuff," and I'd get mad with him, too. If I lose a match, I don't want to have anything to do with the sports pages the next day. I don't know why; maybe because it's only one person's interpretation of the performance. I don't want to believe what some other person thinks about me. I don't like it when they overdramatize and write, "One of the greatest players that ever lived." I know in my mind what I have to improve, what my weaknesses are, my strengths and achievements. I don't need anyone else to tell me.'

However, what Chris didn't realize that Wimbledon until it was too late was that when she walked on to the Centre Court for the final against Evonne Cawley she was seriously underestimating her opponent.

The day before in the semi-finals she had sensationally defeated Martina Navratilova, the no. 1 seed and the girl who had destroyed her Wimbledon hopes in the finals in the two previous years.

The semi-final match had been on one of the only fine days

during a rainy championship and Chris played tentatively at the beginning, losing the first set 4–6. Grass was Martina's preferred surface and Chris was down a set and losing the match in the second when she hit a lucky shot which dribbled over the net. It proved to be the turning point of the match and the momentum changed. Chris started to come into the net, flexibly changing her tactics because she wasn't winning with her usual baseline game. She won with a final score of 4–6, 6–4, 6–2.

'I was on a high; it was a real thrill for me to beat Martina and I thought after that I'd win the tournament because my record against Evonne was excellent.'

John and Chris went out to dinner with his parents at the Café Royale in Wimbledon and Chris enjoyed the evening, relieved because she had eliminated her main threat, the no. 1 seed, in a terrific match that day and she was confident about the final.

Unfortunately, because it had been such a wet Wimbledon, the ladies didn't have the usual day off in between the semi-finals and the final so Chris found herself relatively unprepared mentally for the match against Evonne which took place the following afternoon. The Australian took the first set 6–1 and streaked ahead to a 3–0 lead in the second set before Chris started to find some momentum. But then it started to rain and the players had to leave the court. As she waited in the ladies' locker room for the rain to pass Chris took a call from Jimmy Connors. 'He tried to psych me up and said, "You've got to start; you've got to get going now." He was trying to say, "What's going on out there? Start playing your game." That meant a lot to me. Even though we'd broken up we still supported each other and once in a while he'd watch my matches and I'd watch his and we'd really want the other to win. His call gave me a lot of support.'

Chris went back on court buoyed up by her conversation with Jimmy. She reached a 6–5 lead in the second set but then Evonne broke her serve to force a tie-breaker and won the match.

'If I'd won the tie-breaker it might have been a different story. I couldn't believe I'd lost,' Chris said, remembering her feelings after the match. However, it didn't take long for her to recover with her champion's rubber-ball reaction to defeat – so different to John's when he lost. 'The great champions don't hide when they lose; they go out on the practice court and pledge never to let it happen again,' said John.

Chris resolved there and then to work all out to win Wimbledon the following year. But she couldn't persuade John to resolve to do something constructive after his defeat by Buster Mottram which had left him so despondent. 'When I've lost a match before I've always thought, "I've got a few things to work on."' John said. 'But everyone's playing so much better; anyone can beat me now.'

John may not have been able to make any strong resolutions after his defeats, though he did take them more easily than Chris (but then he had had infinitely more practice at it). He would go quiet and pensive for about an hour then get up out of his easy chair declaring that it was only a tennis match and make plans to go out to dinner or to see a movie.

Chris would sulk for days after a bad defeat, playing and re-playing the crucial points over and over in her mind. She could afford that indulgence because she only lost three or four times a year. In 1980, her record was even better than that: since her comeback in the Italian Open in May she had only lost one match.

After Wimbledon her next victory was in the US Clay Courts Championship where she beat fifteen-year-old Andrea Jaeger 6–4, 6–3. The daughter of an ex-boxer who had emigrated from Switzerland to the United States, Jaeger, like Austin, was a teenage prodigy out of the Evert mould. She even had Chris's hallmark – the two-handed backhand. She had exploded on to the international scene that year taking the Avon Futures title in Las Vegas four months before her fifteenth birthday, which made her the youngest ever pro to win a tournament.

But at the back of Chris's mind since she had returned to full-time tennis was her next encounter with her other youthful rival, Tracy Austin, whom she hadn't played since the beginning of the year when Tracy had notched up five crushing victories over Chris without the loss of a set.

Mr Evert saw the Tracy threat more philosophically than his daughter: 'I accepted that Tracy had just come on strong and I felt there was a possibility that she might keep it up, but there again she might not. The more Chris played her, the more she could play on equal terms with her.'

Chris – the loser in the Italian and United States Opens, the Porsche Grand Prix in Stuttgart and two Colgate defeats at the beginning of 1980 before her break – had elevated Tracy sub-consciously into the 'unbeatable' category. In addition Evonne had beaten Tracy at Wimbledon and then Chris in the final.

'I felt Tracy could only get better,' Chris said. The one weakness in Tracy's game which she felt that she could exploit was her lack of flexibility. 'I knew that if I could drop shot her, bring her up to the net, run her around, lob her and use tactics Evonne would use against her, putting her in awkward situations, I could win.'

But there were plenty of cynics at the US Open at Flushing Meadow in 1980 who believed that old champions never come back. They were betting that the twenty-five-year-old from Fort Lauderdale was going downhill while sixteen-year-old Tracy could only get better. However, it wouldn't be the first time that Chris had turned up trumps, and with sensational style, too.

In the semi-finals the pressure was on Tracy. She was the defending champion, top seed and no. 1. Chris well knew the feeling. 'There's a lot of pressure because you've got to beat everybody and every time you lose it's a major upset. Other people's expectations of you, as well as your own, build up and you're a failure in the public's eyes if you lose. On the other hand, you have an inner confidence because you've beaten so many players and you feel that everyone should be intimidated by you – that's an advantage.'

On a day at Flushing Meadow made gloomy by persistent light drizzle, that advantage took Tracy to a 4–0 lead in the first set. Ron Samuels, who was watching the game with his then-wife, 'Wonder Woman' Lynda Carter, Mrs Evert and John, cupped his hands round his mouth, stood up and yelled, 'OK, so the match is only just beginning now.'

It was Ron's way of jolting Chris out of the paralysis she seemed to be suffering caused by her nerves. She got the message and pepped up her game, but couldn't win the first set which Tracy took 6–4.

Chris had always contended that being no. 2 means a little less pressure and a greater incentive to pursue and attack. That's how she played in the second and third sets, exploiting her teenaged opponent's weaknesses by unnervingly varying her tactics. Everything she tried worked. From her promising 4–0 lead in the first set Tracy could only win four out of the next twenty games and an ecstatic Chris was through to the final, 4–6, 6–1, 6–1.

It was more than a win. She had eradicated the threat of the 'little girl who could do everything better than me'; she'd punctured the Austin invincibility for ever. 'It only takes one win to prove a player is not invincible; if you can do it once you can do it again,' Chris said.

Overwhelmed by the victory, Chris went to the referee's shed by the court and dialled Fort Lauderdale. 'Dad, I won,' she announced and an exclamation of 'That's great,' bounced back down the line from her father. Half an hour later, though, Mr Evert doubted whether he'd heard right. 'I went upstairs,' he remembered, 'and called the stadium back to ask who won.' The result confirmed, he was doubly thrilled by Chris's win. 'It was really touching because none of us expected it; she hadn't had that bad a summer but it hadn't been that good either.'

Tearfully Chris hugged her mother as they left the National Tennis Center but it was John who was the steadying influence: this was only the semi-final; tomorrow she was to meet Hana Mandlikova in the final. The important thing was to learn from her experience at Wimbledon where after her semi-final triumph over Martina she had misjudged the final and lost to Evonne Cawley. Chris calmed down and harnessed all her resources for the next day's match, utilizing the self-confidence which the semi-final win had given her, rather than enjoying its glory. She left the pile of congratulatory telegrams unopened, and ignored the magnums of champagne in their ice buckets and the messages affixed to the extravagant bouquets of flowers.

Her dedication paid off and twenty-four hours later she had a double reason for a celebration – her fifth US Open crown. Hana had been 2–4 down in the opening set but fought back to win it 7–5. Chris didn't let this throw her, just as the loss of the first set against Tracy hadn't, and in the next two sets she repeated her semi-final score of 6–1, 6–1. Elated at the end of the match she threw her arms in the air and jumped for joy – expressing more feelings and emotion than she normally does whatever the result.

This was no ordinary victory. She was the world's no. 1 for the year, Tracy would never again be invulnerable, and it was the climax of her comeback. Victory tasted sweeter the second time around. 'Had any win meant more?' she was asked in the press conference. Her simple 'No' said it all.

That win launched the post-Tracy phase of Chris's career. 'If I'd lost, it would have brought me down mentally. I'd had a few jolts and I needed that match more than anything. The win gave me renewed confidence. I thought: "I've already improved ten per cent; maybe now I can improve another ten per cent." It gave me more incentive to work hard. Everyone had doubted me that year so it made me feel good that I came through when my back was up against the wall.'

Although John has said that some of his happiest moments were sharing Chris's Grand Slam title wins, her victories couldn't compensate wholly for the misery his own career was continuing to cause.

John hadn't even been able to get through the qualifying rounds and into the US Open where Chris had put up those two exceptional performances against Tracy and Hana. The failure was another on his list of defeats of which the cause was self-destruction. He had played American college student Leif Shiras, a shaggy-looking version of him who was later seen as a similar heart-throb by British schoolgirls when in 1984 at Queen's Club, London, he sensationally defeated Ivan Lendl. Since then Leif has frequently been called John's look-alike and even been asked by John's fans for his autograph. 'I hope your wife wins Wimbledon,' one well-wisher once told him. But in 1980 Leif Shiras was unknown and when Chris asked John who he was playing, he'd replied, 'Someone who shouldn't be a problem.' Unfortunately, on court on the day, it was John who not so much couldn't as wouldn't try to play. He switched himself once again into the now sadly familiar cycle and tossed away a winnable match.

Chris watched in horror as John, who had a comfortable lead, slumped his shoulders, annoyed at himself for one poor shot, and said, 'Stuff it; I don't want to be out here.' Later he admitted, 'I virtually just started slamming balls into the fence and looked at Chris who was getting more and more upset. I could see she was in tears.'

Chris was mortified: 'It was so obvious he wasn't trying. He wasn't moving for the balls or even going through the motions. He'd quit mentally and physically.' Ron Samuels had flown in from California especially to support John. He felt badly let down by his lack of effort and told him so in no uncertain terms after the match.

Chris, exasperated, spoke her mind: 'I'm not coming to watch you again unless you try. You're meant to be a professional tennis player but you're not acting like one; you're playing gutless tennis.' Her own very high competitive standards were thoroughly offended by John's throwing another match away.

John felt that he was punishing himself for not being committed to the game. 'I didn't want to face up to the fact that people were saying, "There's a guy who was ranked in the twenties – look at him now, down in the 300s." Even when I thought I might make a comeback I never really wanted to make the full commitment. I didn't want to go into the qualifying rounds and say, "Here I am, I'm trying my hardest." I wanted to be able to justify losing to myself and others by giving the appearance that I wasn't really interested and wasn't bothering. In a lot of ways my whole career has been taking the easy option. People sometimes said to me that it was fine if I didn't want to play tennis and that I should do something else, but I'd look around and think what can I do? What do I want to do? Deep down I knew I wanted to play, but I just didn't want to commit myself.'

Neither Ron nor Chris could stomach any more matches like the one they'd just seen and made John swear that it would be the last time. 'He promised us he'd never do it again, that he wouldn't walk on court unless he was going to try one hundred per cent; but he'd done it repeatedly and could not seem to get out of the downward spiral,' Chris said.

It was sixteen months since Chris, as a new bride, had watched the first instance of John's losing syndrome at the Foro Italico in the 1979 Italian Open and she'd said then, 'I can take a couple of these but no more.' John was now well into borrowed time.

As the Lloyds packed to leave Flushing Meadow at the conclusion of the Open there was the usual discrepancy in their fortunes. Chris had been a complete success, acclaimed as a born-again champion; she was commanding more respect than ever, had justified her sabbatical and proved that the old winning magic was back, that the teenager clones would have a difficult time ousting her.

She was also on her way to the hundredth tournament win of her career when she beat Andrea Jaeger in the final of the Lynda Carter Maybelline Women's Tennis Classic at Deerfield Beach, Florida, the following month.

In contrast, John's ranking had slumped to no. 356 and his malaise seemed to be worsening, even though he delighted in Chris's victories and no one could criticize his creditable support role. This was publicly recognized by *World Tennis* magazine in a photographic feature titled 'Best in a supporting role: some of the stars and their valuable helpmates', when John appeared in the company of Jimmy Connors's wife Patti, Bjorn Borg's wife Mariana and Rosie Casals's dog Midnight. The questions remained, how long could John, his wife and their marriage tolerate these perpetual failures? And how were they changing his personality – whatever the credit he was getting for helping Chris?

CHAPTER SEVEN

1981
Chris's High, John's Low

No tennis professional could have demonstrated finer tennis than Chris Lloyd in her magnificent 6–0, 6–0 victory in the final of the Murjani-WTA Championship at Amelia Island, Florida in April 1981.

John and Chris had just signed up as touring pros at the beautiful ocean-front tennis resort on the Atlantic coast and Chris made sure that her debut was vintage tennis.

Her opponent, on whom she inflicted this pulverizing forty-seven minute whitewash, was Martina Navratilova. The one-sided match left the loser close to tears and the defeat proved a turning point in Martina's career, inspiring her to begin training seriously. Chris remembered how it happened.

'That match was the first time I had met Nancy Lieberman, who Martina had got together with that week. I heard later that she had told Martina after the match: "That was disgraceful. Why don't you decide to get the best out of your potential? You're going to have to work hard and train hard. You should have more pride in your performance."

'From then on it was Nancy who really trained her, and got her into great athletic shape. I think that in a sense she was living through Martina, channelling everything into her because her own basketball career had ended.'

Chris had first played Martina eight years before at Akron, Ohio in 1973, two years before the young Czech had defected to the United States. Chris had beaten the dark-haired girl 7–6, 6–3, but Martina had made quite an impression on her.

'I realized that physically she was very strong and muscular. She was the first left-handed woman I'd played on the circuit. I'd never heard of her or seen her play so I was shocked by her big serve which was probably one of the best, even at that young age. She also served and volleyed which for someone young was rare; I was used to players being baseliners when they were teenagers. I also noticed she was very emotional and vocal – she whined a lot on court. She was pretty inconsistent from the back-court so I knew that as soon as I could get her there I had her. I remember thinking that she was still very young and could become dangerous if she was more consistent. But then you can never tell; she could just have been a flash in the pan.'

Since Akron, Chris had played her about forty times, but none of her victories had been such a decimating loss for Martina.

Chris likened her to John in that they had both wasted a lot of talent for several years, but then in 1981 Martina suddenly became determined to make up for lost time.

Unfortunately the same could not be said for John that spring. Even though he'd spent two years in the wilderness he had neither the motivation nor the confidence to mount a full-scale revival of his career.

The widening gap between the Lloyds's tennis careers precipitated the first cracks in their marriage. Tennis had brought them together; it was their occupation and what their marriage was based on. Problems in tennis were accompanied by difficulties in their relationship.

This was their third year of marriage and a more settled time than the honeymoon of the first and the upheavals they'd had in the second. After their April wedding they'd spent the remainder of 1979 enjoying the first heady days of married life, happy to push tennis aside.

In 1980 John had supported Chris during her period of indecision about whether to stay in the game. He'd been with her for much of her sabbatical and worked with her afterwards as she battled her way back to defeat Tracy and regain the no. 1 position.

She, in turn, had travelled with him to try and inspire him to raise his game, but it had been to no avail. With John embarrassed about the state of his own tennis and humiliating her when she came and watched, she could only focus her attention more and more on her own game which inevitably meant they were separated for longer periods while playing different tournaments.

John had received the unwelcome New Year's present of being dropped from the Lawn Tennis Association's official British rankings for the first time in eight years. Since 1973 John had always been in the top ten and his omission confirmed the alarming extent to which his game had disintegrated. In the ATP computer rankings he was no. 356 in the world.

On a purely pragmatic point it also meant that he had no hope of being accepted straight into any tournament but would have to rely on wildcards – invitations at the disposal of the tournament organizers – and then fight his way through the qualifying rounds. It was of little comfort and did nothing for John's morale that often the reason tournament promoters benevolently granted him a wildcard was because he was Chris Evert's husband.

He was invited to play at the Indoor Championships in Philadelphia in January but lost in the qualifying rounds to American college student Jay Lapidus in under an hour with a display which indicated the extent to which his confidence had dwindled and reflected his lack of match play. 'There was the all-too-familiar welter of rushed shots,' the *Daily Telegraph* commented on the 6–3, 6–2 defeat.

More disappointment was in store for John in March when Britain's Davis Cup captain, Paul Hutchins, dropped him from the team to play Italy, the first time in four years that neither David nor John played for Britain. Hutchins explained his reasoning: 'In 1979 I picked John to play Spain when he hadn't won a match in seventeen and my gamble paid off when he beat Manuel Orantes. But he was playing regularly then, he is not now.'

John realized that on his present form, after such a terrible start to the year, Hutchins couldn't possibly justify including him in the team, but he was annoyed at some of the comments he read in newspapers which seemed to assume that he was finished.

'Basically it was like being swept under the carpet. I felt it could have been handled a bit more tactfully.'

Plunging down to the qualifying rounds, because of his low computer ranking, seemed to deplete any incentive John might have had left in him. 'I felt like I didn't deserve to be in the main draw any more. Even when I did qualify and get into a tournament I'd lose in the first round every time because I subconsciously felt that was where I belonged. It was a place where I could still play a few matches yet hide without being up with the big guns.'

The further down John's spirits sank the more critical he was of himself. The qualifying rounds are fiercely competitive even for the up-and-coming hungry youngsters but an especially unpalatable trial for the husband of the women's no. 1 whose playing fortunes had temporarily hit hard times.

'We'd go to these qualifyings and I'd feel a bit out of place, flying first class, staying in nice hotels because of Chris when the other guys were scrounging for pennies and eating their takeaway meals. The qualifying is an unbelievably tough circuit – dog eat dog – with some players who would do anything to win. It got to the stage where I asked Chris not to come and watch me play. I think she was relieved in a lot of ways because when she did come ninety per cent of the time I wouldn't try in my matches. It was very embarrassing for her because there'd be reporters there just because it was Chris and I.'

Looking across the net John would read the expression on his opponent's face, which said, 'What's this guy doing here, taking the bread out of our mouths?'

A lot of people asked John why he was continuing to play when he didn't need to financially, and the press made plenty of sarcastic remarks about him.

'The newspapers in England and Australia – the two worst – love to cut people down when they're at their lowest point. I read what they said sometimes, I suppose I shouldn't, and that made me think that the easiest thing to do would be to leave the circuit and be Chris's manager or do something different. But I didn't want to do that; I still thought I could get back to a certain level. It wasn't that I particularly wanted to prove them wrong. I wanted more than anything to prove myself.'

He was so cross in the following months that his name wasn't among the possible candidates for future Davis Cup teams that when he battled successfully through the first round of the GMC Moben Kitchens tournament in Manchester in June he declared that he wouldn't play even if he was asked. 'I felt if that's the way they think I won't make myself available.'

It was an unhappy and de-stabilizing cycle; a rollercoaster of catastrophies and encouraging signs of progress but which John found difficult to sustain and nurture. In the early summer he had a burst of moderate success and his computer ranking crept up to no. 220. Tennis watchers dared to whisper predictions of a Lloyd 'mini revival'.

While Chris was playing at the French Open John got a wildcard entry into the Stella Artois tournament at London's Queen's Club which he justified when he beat Frenchman Christophe Roger-Vasselin 6–2, 7–6 and earned some compliments for his splendid serving.

In Paris, Chris had hoped to make the French Open an Evert family affair with her parents and sister Clare at the tournament as a present for Clare's graduation from eighth-grade. Mr Evert, who loathes big crowds and all the attention and fuss of major tournaments and gets very nervous watching Chris, had agreed to fly over but Mrs Evert had her doubts and suspected that he would get cold feet at the last moment.

'Jimmy had never been to the French Open,' she remembered. 'He said, "We'd better go and get me some clothes; I don't want Chrissie to be ashamed of me." So we went and bought some Gucci loafers, a blazer, pants and suits and all that. As the time drew closer he said, "Maybe I'd better not come; my blood pressure might get high and I don't want to be a burden to anybody." I could see him working himself up to not coming. Then he said, "I'll go and have my blood pressure taken", and he went and it was high, which I thought was psychosomatic.'

Mrs Evert and Clare went to the tournament without him and it was an eventful fortnight off court as well as on. Chris and Bjorn Borg were made International Tennis Federation Champions and attended the awards dinner, but it wasn't the only thing they had in common: they had also both put in forthright complaints to the manager of the Hilton Hotel, where they were staying, about the disturbances made by the entourages of foreign royalty. Chris had been deprived of sleep by chirping birds owned by the brother of the King of Saudi Arabia and Bjorn's nights were disturbed by the thuds and gyrations of another royal king's belly dancers in action in the room above his.

Chris, who was top seed, beat Virginia Wade 6–3, 6–0 and Virginia Ruzici 6–4, 6–4 on her way to face no. 3 seed Hana Mandlikova in the semi-finals. Chris had watched Hana play in Paris and had an inkling that she could be a threat to her chances of taking the Grand Slam title, even though in the best part of two hundred singles matches on clay she had only lost once – to Tracy Austin at the 1979 Italian Open.

Because of the tension, Chris played well below her usual standard and exited from her sixth French Open in the semi-finals with a score of 7–5, 6–4, beaten by the eventual champion.

'Hana simply played too well,' was Chris's comment on her Paris defeat, which also ended her second clay court winning streak at sixty-four in a row.

It was a bad loss. Shortly afterwards Chris developed a swollen tibia (the bone leading up to the knee), defaulted from a grass-court tournament in Surrey and went to recuperate at John's Wimbledon flat. Her spirits were gloomy owing to the French loss and her injury. 'I didn't play for four days. I just sat and watched TV and felt really depressed.'

When she had recovered, hitting with John and working out with Dennis Ralston and a practice squad of other Wimbledon entrants on grass courts at Holland Park, London, rejuvenated Chris and hunger for a Wimbledon victory began to flow through her.

She practised for four hours a day doing strenuous two-players-hitting-to-one drills – a very concentrated form of practice – and playing endless sets to perfect her match tactics.

Both Lloyds went into Wimbledon with positive hopes about their prospects – Chris with an iron determination to win the tournament and John itching to avenge the humiliating defeat by Buster Mottram which he had suffered there twelve months earlier, at a nadir in his career.

In the opening round John fought through five tough sets against Phil Dent of Australia 6–4, 3–6, 4–6, 6–3, 6–4 and looked a different player from the one who let one bad mistake wreck his chances in a match. In the second round he put up a very respectable performance against Argentina's Jose Luis Clerc, the no. 9 seed, in a four-set match on the Centre Court. Although John took the first set, Clerc won 4–6, 6–3, 7–6, 6–4.

The Wimbledon draw favoured Chris's fortunes. She beat Pam Shriver in one semi-final and Hana Mandlikova eliminated Chris's main threat, Martina Navratilova, in the other.

Chris knew then that her third Wimbledon title was a possibility. On the day of the final Hana was suffering from a psychological let-down after her jubilant 7–5, 4–6, 6–1 semi-final triumph over Martina. Her wandering attention had communicated itself to Chris when they were both sitting in the players' waiting room waiting to go on to the Centre Court and she'd asked who Maureen Connolly was while examining a photograph of her which hung on the wall.

Chris had actually once been a ballgirl for the three-times Wimbledon champion at the age of about eight when Maureen had played an exhibition match with Chris's father in Fort Lauderdale, and she enlightened Hana about 'Little Mo's' tennis achievements. 'She was my idol back in those days. It was the first time I came into contact with anybody really good,' Chris remembered.

As Chris walked with Hana from the waiting room and out under the Royal Box she scanned Hana for clues to her hunger. She detected that the overwhelming will to win which had propelled Hana to victory over her in the semi-final of the French Open, and Sylvia Hanika of West Germany in the final, was absent.

On the Centre Court that Saturday the gifted but erratic youngster was outclassed and Chris won her third Wimbledon victory with a 6–2, 6–2 score.

Chris later explained her strategy for Hana's benefit. 'There's more to being in the final than playing well. Hana thought that maybe you could win on talent alone, but you've got to go out there and be gutsy and use your head. She really didn't use her head at all. She was making errors and playing sloppily, so she didn't deserve to win.'

For Chris, victory was a reward for sheer hard work, compensation for having been runner-up for the three previous years, and it put her name on the champions' board for 1981 in addition to 1974 and 1976. It also meant so much more than her previous win because she had John to share it with.

It was a record, too. In seven matches at the tournament she had only lost twenty-six games and was the first player since Billie Jean King in 1967 to win Wimbledon without the loss of a set.

After the match Chris and John met Lady Diana Spencer, who was due to marry the Prince of Wales in St Paul's Cathedral three weeks later, in the Royal Box. Much to John's embarrassment, Chris took the liberty of telling the future Princess of Wales how much she regretted that Prince Charles was not a tennis fan and didn't come to Wimbledon.

In 1974 at the Wimbledon Ball Chris had opened the dancing with Jimmy Connors; in 1976 with Bjorn Borg; but in 1981 it was only the female champion who attended the traditional gathering at the Savoy – John McEnroe, who had defeated Bjorn Borg 4–6, 7–6, 7–6, 6–4 in an epic men's final, didn't turn up.

He had been a controversial player for the whole fortnight, owing to his odious on-court behaviour. Acres of newsprint had reported and condemned his yelling out, 'You're a disgrace to mankind,' which the umpire of his match had taken to refer to himself and had handed out a conduct warning. In another match McEnroe had shouted his infamous utterance, 'You guys are the absolute pits of the world,' which resulted in his being penalized for obscenity because the umpire thought he'd said 'piss'. The All England Club imposed a £5,000 fine on John McEnroe which was later reduced to £2,500 by the Pro Council Administrator, Marshall Happer, and seven months later overturned completely by an appeal panel.

At the dinner Chris was in the unenviable position of being the female champion in a ballroom full of people anxiously waiting to see whether her unpredictable male counterpart would honour them with his presence. When it became clear that he would not it was left to her to try and redeem the occasion and, after consulting with husband John, she loosened everyone up with a few jokes, delivered with her customary aplomb and style.

'Sir Brian Burnett (Chairman of the All England Club Committee) has told me that I must make two speeches, one for myself and one for what's his name, but I don't want to use his vocabulary,' she addressed the dinner and apologized for John's failure to attend.

At the time Chris had no way of knowing about the behind-the-scenes drama which surrounded John McEnroe's invitation to the dinner and his decision not to attend, but nevertheless he was very displeased about her speech for two champions and apology on his behalf.

'I meant what I said to be funny but he didn't like my apologizing for him not being there and got very upset about it. I explained to him that it was just meant as a joke but he said I had no right to apologize, it was none of my business. He's really sensitive and I think he took it the wrong way. We talked about it when I saw him at the US Open and he said he was still upset about it. Now when people ask me about his behaviour I reply that his on-court antics go too far but I try to explain that he has a less well-known good side, too.

'John represents the United States in Davis Cup and he plays a lot of exhibition matches for charity. I don't think that as no. 1 he sets a good example for young kids to follow, but he does have positive points which many people don't know about.'

Chris, who has a reputation for being the best behaved player in the world, can understand why some people blow up on court in the heat of battle when there's a ranking and so much money at stake. She says that her impeccable on-court demeanour is the result of her upbringing and her early experiences on the circuit.

'My parents brought me up to be a good sport. Good sportsmanship was as important, if not more so, than winning or losing. When I started on the circuit, before I was accepted by the other players, the whole tour used to gang up and cheer for my opponent. These things combined to make me the way I am on court. I keep everything inside; I don't show any emotions, and don't let them know my feelings are hurt.'

John, though he acknowledges that McEnroe does overdo it, can also see why some players explode in anger, especially about incompetent officials. 'Sometimes you get umpires who aren't ex-players and who don't know how to interpret a match, but just read out the rule book. They really shouldn't be umpiring matches at a high level of competition, because they make mistakes which could conceivably cost you a match. It's not surprising that some players go berserk.'

John, who is also a devoted soccer fan, is quick to condemn the different standards that are found on court and pitch. 'A referee will quite often leave it when a player, whom he has just cautioned, turns round and swears at him. If referees booked players every time they swore about twenty of them would be sent off in each match.'

Chris's jokes at the Wimbledon dinner were a public sample of her great sense of humour which makes her such entertaining company in private. 'You just never stop laughing when Chris is around,' one friend said. 'She's so quick witted, you can see her mind ticking over when you're talking and you know that in a split second she'll come up with an incisive one-liner which will have everyone in fits of laughter.'

Chris thinks her capacity to entertain originated from her shyness as a child. 'When I was funny I started getting attention. I still think one of the best feelings is making everyone have a good laugh. In that way I'm glad that I'm not a great beauty because it makes you work to develop your personality. If you're the best looking girl in the classroom then you don't bother.'

Chris's sense of fun once delighted a crowd in Salt Lake City where John, Vitas Gerulaitis, Billie Jean King and Kathy Jordan were playing an exhibition match. Before the game started members of the public were invited to take part in a fast-serving competition to see who could return one of Vitas's serves. No one succeeded so Chris, who was there to watch John, strolled on court in high heels and hit the ball way up into the stands, to cheers from the crowd.

Chris handles press conferences and interviews in the same style. 'What are your thoughts on that?' a journalist vaguely asked her in one post-match press conference. 'About what, the match?' she flashed back. At the Australian Open in 1984 another journalist announced that he'd run naked down the road outside Kooyong if one of his favourite cricket players was dropped from the Australian team. Chris heard about it and when the player was dropped she walked into another post-match press conference and before taking the first question she inquired, 'Is Bruce here?'

Her lively sense of humour comes over well on television, too. On a British breakfast TV programme the presenter introduced a film-clip of 'John and you in action.' 'Ah, oh,' Chris responded with perfect timing and a sexy expression.

Thanking Tommy Tucker for his speech to dedicate a clay court to her at Mission Hills Country Club in Palm Springs, she noticed that the plaque resembled one on a tombstone. 'But then I'm getting used to these old age jokes now I'm over thirty,' she laughed, and the crowd with her.

From Wimbledon, Chris's busy summer schedule took her back across the Atlantic to Illinois to play in the Wightman Cup where two singles victories over Virginia Wade and Sue Barker kept her 'no losses' record intact. The United States routed Britain with a seven-rubbers-to-love whitewash.

Just before the US Open Chris played in the Canadian Open in Toronto where she lost to Tracy Austin in the final after a demanding three-set semi-final against Andrea Jaeger.

She also had the unnerving experience of a death-threat being made against her. Although she wasn't told about it until after the final, the security precautions were rather unsettling.

'I was staying with a good friend, Loretta DeCarli, and when she drove me to the tournament I thought it was a bit curious because she practically drove the car right on to the court instead of parking in the usual place. Then during the match I looked up and saw a policeman in each aisle, which I thought was weird.'

It was Chris's second bad experience of this sort. Some years before, in mid-flight, the two men sitting in front of her had turned round and identified themselves as FBI agents, saying they were there to protect her because there'd been a death-threat.

'They said an anonymous caller had threatened to kill a famous athlete on this flight. I was the only one on it so they told me that when we landed I was to walk fast, keep my head down, get into the police car and go straight to the hotel. It was really scary because there's nothing you can do on an aeroplane in the middle of a flight.'

With the US Open at Flushing Meadow at the end of August only a week or so away, Chris joined coach Dennis Ralston and John at Kiawah Island, North Carolina for some practice sessions just as they had practised in July at Holland Park in London for Wimbledon.

Unfortunately John couldn't find the same kind of determination which had carried Chris to ultimate victory over Hana at Wimbledon, nor could he even muster the effort he'd put into his own singles matches. He was not at his competitive best and it looked as though his mini-revival had fizzled out.

John admitted afterwards that he was irritated during the training and lacked motivation. He longed to pull out of the tournament altogether. 'I thought that I would play it as my last tournament and prayed that I would be drawn against someone who was an average, middle-of-the-road player so I could play on an outside court, lose the match and that would be the end of that.'

John's prayers about staying on the sidelines weren't answered. The result of the draw meant that he was to play top seed Jimmy Connors in a match that would open the Centenary US Championships.

'I didn't want to play Jimmy because he always tries so hard and I knew it was going to be a centre court match.'

The tennis apart, the match had all the makings of a marvellous TV soap-opera-like publicity stunt: America's no. 1 watches her macho, tennis ace, ex-fiancé challenge her good-looking, blond, 'Mr Nice Guy' husband whose tennis had never equalled Jimmy's and whose game was now in serious trouble. 'Jimmy seemed to have an intense determination to beat John. Maybe he took this match a little more personally than others,' Chris remembered.

The match was seventy-nine minutes of humiliation for John who spent the entire time willing a crevass to appear in the court and gobble him up. Jimmy took the first set 6–0 with the loss of only seven points.

'I must try and get a game on the board,' John kept repeating to himself, loathing every moment, his legs feeling like lead. At 2–0 down in the second set rather than improving and getting into the match he found himself playing progressively worse. The New York crowd, never particularly sympathetic, displayed their displeasure at the poor spectacle by whistling.

'It was awful; it was such a bad match and I was getting thumped,' John said. His discomfort increased. 'It might have looked as though I wasn't trying – in fact I was trying hard but I was frozen and couldn't move.'

John lost the second set 6–0 and just wanted to get off the court. Chris's heart went out to him, knowing that although she and Jimmy had been married to John and Patti respectively for over two years the match still had an extra dimension.

Utterly outclassed and fearing the ignominy of a whitewash, John looked up and caught a glimpse of his friend Ron shaking a clenched fist at him, but it was to little avail. He went two games down in the third set, having lost fourteen games in a row. Then he won two games to level at 2–all, but that was all Connors was going to allow him and he swept the next four games to finish the match mercilessly.

'After the match I was in tears inside. I felt totally and utterly humiliated, totally and utterly scared. I remember saying to Chris, "That's it, my last match. I don't ever want to play in front of a crowd again." '

It was another occasion when Chris's support role consisted largely of talking John out of quitting the game for good.

'I felt I wasn't going anywhere and it was time to stop playing.

It was always Chris who sat me down and talked me out of it. She said, "Don't do it, you'd be a fool if you did." She had a lot of faith in my ability; she could see the talent that I had and that I would be stupid to stop playing before I'd fulfilled my potential. A number of times I used to sit there and say, "You don't know what you're talking about, I'm finished." '

Fortunately for John when he lost in Grand Slam events Chris would usually be playing on until at least the semi-finals and usually the finals at the end of the tournament, so he couldn't submerge himself in his own problems to the extent that they distracted her. Frequently it was that 'cooling off' period which stopped him quitting, until the next time he lost when he would say, 'That's the end of it' and Chris would step in again.

'She was the one who pushed me to keep going. If she'd said, "OK, I think it's time you stopped," I probably would just have given up, but she never said that.'

A fortnight later at the US Open it was the New York crowd which inadvertently influenced the outcome of Chris's semi-final against Martina Navratilova. Chris was leading 4–2 in the third set when the match was held up for ten minutes while fighting spectators were removed. When play was resumed she lost four games in a row, the set and the match. 'It was one of those matches which could have gone either way. I remember thinking maybe if there hadn't been a fight it might have been different,' Chris said.

Despite the fact that she was beaten in the final by Tracy Austin 1–6, 7–6, 7–6, Martina's form indicated just how much Nancy Lieberman's training had done for her since Chris had defeated her at Amelia Island earlier in 1981. 'She was more consistent, she was playing better tennis, seemed in better shape and was more hungry,' Chris judged. It would be another year before Martina started her winning run over Chris but the foundation for her future invincibility had been laid.

The tennis circus moved on to Australia for the Open in Melbourne, before which Chris beat Martina in the final of the New South Wales women's tournament in Sydney 6–4, 2–6, 6–1, making it two matches-all out of their four encounters in 1981.

But the Sydney win augured badly for Chris's second final in two weeks against Martina in the Australian Open in Kooyong in Melbourne. It was a very close fought match: in the tense first set tiebreaker the score was 4–4 then Chris took the next three points. Martina took the second set 6–4. In the third set Chris was 1–5 down and scraped back to 5–5. Chris was serving at 30–40 and Martina won the break after a fierce volleying exchange at the net. That was the turning point: Martina had two match points. She lost the first and won the second.

This match had been a cliffhanger and afterwards the result preyed on Chris's mind. It was also her second attempt to win the Australian title and her second failure. With an eye always on the next time she resolved 'third time lucky'.

In Australia John forecast 1982 as his make-or-break year, saying then: 'After nine years of playing in tournaments it's tough having to qualify. If by this time next year I'm still in the same situation I will almost certainly retire. I would think that someone was trying to tell me something.'

John's erratic career with its high failure rate was starting to take its toll on his personality, and Chris remembers that John was wasting away and wasn't happy with himself.

He retreated into his shell and took refuge in his favourite form of escapism – long hours in front of the video or the television. Finding a video acceptable to both husband and wife isn't easy, since Chris loathes horror: 'John usually goes to watch horror films by himself. If he puts on a video and we're sitting down together I'll leave in the middle of the film because it doesn't really interest me. I don't like to be scared. If people creep up behind me I almost have a heart attack, and I hate the dark – I always have to have a light on when I go to sleep.'

Scaring others John regards as an essential part of the fun. 'Our friends Ron and Kathy don't like horror films so sometimes I make them watch one. It's hilarious because I know when the good parts are coming and I can watch them getting really scared.'

John is quite choosy about his videos: 'I like them to be classy horrors, if there are such things, not just blood and guts.'

John's obsession for video nasties mystifies even his wife. 'He's a contradiction: he's a very gentle man but he loves watching boxing, scary movies with sex and violence and reading about gory things in the newspapers. Yet he can't be in a hospital room, can't bear the sight of blood in real life and hates to have an injection. It's as though he likes seeing it happening to others, but not himself.'

There was high drama in the Lloyd household once when a guest, who shared John's taste in videos, attempted to slow motion the most outrageous parts of the film *Caligula*. Being an amateur at the video controls, he pressed the record button by mistake and, to John's dismay, erased the choicest scenes, recording in their place a tame TV show.

Although Chris doesn't share John's taste in videos she is staunchly loyal in her defence of his hobby. 'Because John's such a nice guy he keeps a lot inside himself. He has to have an outlet for all his emotions and watching movies provides one. When people criticize him for his video mania I often say, "If that's an outlet for him, it's the best thing in the world. Why not?" I'll relax by reading a book or talking on the phone to a friend, and if I've a problem I'll talk it out. John relaxes by watching movies. Although he appears to be laid back he's not really; he's quite uptight.'

Football was John's other passion and a sport which he was capable of watching incessantly on television. The phone has been known to ring in the Lloyds's Kingston home with John on the other end in California issuing instructions to housekeeper Jenny Scally how to work the video so she can record *Match of the Day* or some other sporting special for him.

At the Daihatsu Championships in Brighton in October 1983 Chris had beaten Jo Durie in the singles finals and was scheduled with partner Pam Shriver to play Jo and Ann Kiyomura in the doubles final. In the players' lounge in between the two finals, while the players' friends and families chatted and had tea, John made a conspicuous dive for the television to check on the fortunes of his favourite team, Wolves.

'Don't worry about my match,' quipped Chris. He didn't, and it was several games into the first set when he appeared in the stands and swopped the football score with his father in exchange for a bulletin on the progress of the doubles.

Chris doesn't share John's passion although he did make one attempt to change that. 'I've always wanted to try and get Chris involved in football because I like to spend a few hours a day watching it and I felt if I could get her interested in the game she wouldn't get so bored. Finally I said, "Let's go to a match at Wembley." '

Chris and John arrived to see England play Wales and John thought everything augured well when they got the best seats in the house. 'There was a great atmosphere and I cheered as England walked out. Then England played probably the most pathetic match in the history of the world. It was nil–nil with about fifteen minutes to go and my spirits were sinking. There were about five or six drunken, rowdy Welsh supporters sitting a few rows in front of us and they'd been shouting all through the match about how great Wales was. They were spoiling for a fight or at least an argument. Chris nudged me and said, "Are they cheering for the team we want or the others?" and I told her, "No, they're for the others." Chris got mad at them and started cheering for England. They turned round and recognized her and started climbing over the seats to get an autograph. Chris stood her ground and said she definitely wouldn't sign because they'd been cheering for the other side. Frantically John said through gritted teeth, 'Sign the autographs, and don't say a word.' Under her husband's orders Chris scribbled away and John, anxious to avoid any trouble, handed them back smiling.

That experience was Chris's first and last football match.

Relaxation and hobbies were one thing but as John's despondency about his tennis deepened he spent less and less time working at his game and more time vegetating in front of the television.

The differences between husband and wife, which had been surmountable when they were in love, became obstacles once the novelty had worn off. They started to spend more and more time apart, travelling alone to different tournaments, and geographical separation accelerated their drift apart. Tennis had brought them together in the beginning but now John openly wanted to escape from his fading career which seemed even worse when it was compared to Chris's overwhelmingly successful one. The common ground in the relationship was shrinking and it was ominous for their future together. 'Respect is very important in a marriage and I started losing respect for John,' Chris said.

CHAPTER EIGHT

1982-3
The Fairytale
becomes Fiction

Chris's tears in a Los Angeles restaurant were tears of relief, because she and John had finally made the decision to separate for a trial period, but of sadness too that such a decision was necessary. It was December 1983; Chris had arrived from London and John had flown across the Pacific from Australia for a summit meeting on their marriage which would determine whether they tried a separation or went straight for a divorce. They were having dinner in a local restaurant with close friends Ron and Kathy in whose Beverly Hills home they were staying.

John was taking a hard line: 'I'd made up my mind before I met Chris that I wasn't going to accept a separation although that was what Chris wanted. I said, "Either we get back together or we get divorced. If we can't make it, we should call it a day." I was being a bit pig-headed, but then I felt I hadn't done anything wrong.'

John finally agreed to a separation to give Chris time since it would be worth it if it meant there was a chance they could get back together again. He told her, 'If you're mixed up and confused about our marriage let's separate, but if you've made up your mind and separation is just a step before divorce let's get divorced.' He didn't want to be taken for a ride.

Ron, in whom both John and Chris confided, remembered how the Lloyds felt in those dark days. 'I think Chris's parents' reaction had a big impact on her because they're very religious, and were against a divorce.' John had almost resigned himself to the fact that it was over, and was wondering why they should torment each other any more.

Once the decision had been taken, both Chris and John felt the pressure was off, but the emotional impact set in with Chris showing her feelings more outwardly. They spent three or four more days with Ron and Kathy and were like best friends again, doing everything together – going shopping, to the movies and playing tennis. Chris remembered, 'I was crying a lot of the time because although I knew we had to separate I would look across the dinner table at John, who was coping very well, and think he was great. He was still my best friend, but something had left our marriage. I wasn't sure he was the right guy for me for the rest of my life, and I needed time to think about it. I was not leaving John for another man.

'A lot of our relationship had been based on tennis. John had been with me on the tour or I with him and it was convenient because we could practise together and we understood each other's moods during a tournament. In the future there was going to come a time when we'd stop playing so we had to look at one another and ask whether we had other common goals. The truth of the matter is that when you're married to someone you have to like them, want to be with them and want them to be the parent of your child. I hadn't really thought about these things.'

John and Chris had talked on and off all year about separating but it had never been a convenient time for both of them and they had put off making the final decision. Chris remembered, 'When I was ready it was just before Davis Cup and John didn't want any sensational publicity, and when he was ready it wasn't right for me.'

'Let's wait until after Wimbledon,' John suggested when the subject was raised again. Then they talked about splitting up before the US Open in September, but John felt that the publicity which would inevitably accompany a separation announcement would be detrimental to both their performances at Flushing Meadow.

'I was trying to make a comeback and rather selfishly thought it would be tough to have the spotlight turned on us. I thought it would add extra pressure when already I was in rather a fragile state and didn't want anything else to make me worse,' said John.

The wrench of making the decision to separate and actually parting in December 1983 were the final stages in the sad saga of cumulative problems which had put John and Chris's marriage on the rocks as far back as the previous year.

In 1979, Chris had married a tennis player whose hobbies were watching television and videos; within three years the balance had changed and John was glued to the television virtually non-stop mostly as an escape from his failed tennis career.

'I wasn't doing much, just vegetating. I know I spent too much time watching television. I was watching it till two o'clock in the morning and often I would make sure I was back during the day to see a programme I'd already seen twenty times before. If I was going for a run and a programme came on I would watch it to stop doing my run. It was a way of escaping from things. I wasn't facing up to getting on with my job. I didn't have a goal.'

It made Chris, a finely tuned and highly motivated professional as well as a very disciplined person, dismayed and then angry that John could loaf about with no direction, frittering away his life and career.

John's constant vigil in front of the television was one reason the Lloyds's relationship degenerated from a vibrant happy marriage to life in a rut and a stale routine. Friends who visited their Palm Springs home remember Chris would often shout 'Dinner's ready,' from the kitchen, at which John would reply, 'Can I have it out here?' so he didn't have to move his eyes off the screen.

'Watching TV wasn't stimulating for him nor for me. His self-image went down, he became depressed and wasn't contributing anything to the relationship.

'He would also lie in the sun for hours and read magazines. That's fine if you're taking a break or you're on vacation but not as a way of life. I thought this idle recreation was going to develop into a full time occupation – John did it for a year and showed no signs of giving up. Our communication stopped because it was competing with the TV.

'My respect for John had diminished, which worried me. I haven't respected many men in my life, except for my father and him. I would try and tell myself you can't lose respect for him just because he's not doing anything. You should still respect him for the person he is. But it was difficult. After a while I just got angry because he is a great athlete but was wasting his potential. I started thinking that I was going to have to be a little more independent and go my own way, travelling on my own to tournaments and other places.'

John not only didn't want to confront the real state of his tennis, but he also didn't register the signs that his marriage was heading for trouble, despite warnings from friends such as Ron Samuels that he ought to make more of an effort to be assertive and a positive rather than a passive husband.

'John doesn't have a roving eye; he isn't very possessive,' Chris said. 'If I'm talking and laughing with another guy he might come over and I'll introduce him, but if I see him being chatted up by a glamorous blonde I'll go over straight away and find out who she is.'

John had settled into a vacuous routine. 'I just thought everything was fine because my mind was dull. I'd let myself get to a low in my professional career and that clouded everything else, although Chris was giving me lots of hints that she wanted me to be more positive and get involved in her business. I was happy with Chris and loved being with her but I didn't feel a spark because I had my blinkers on.'

Looking back Chris feels that she should have detected John's problem earlier and tried to shake him out of his depression about his game. They gradually drifted apart and no longer made an effort to plan their tournament schedules to be together. When they added it up later they had spent less than a year with each other in five years of marriage.

John remembered, 'If Chris had a good offer for a tournament I'd say, "Yes, you should go," rather than, "No, I want you to be with me that week."'

That was the status quo at the beginning of 1982 when fortuitously John's game started to show signs of a fragile improvement and he found himself back at no. 4 in the official British Lawn Tennis rankings announced in January. In February, in the Congoleum Classic at La Quinta, outside Palm Springs, California, John found a touch of his old form and played well to get through to the third round before being defeated by Raul Ramirez, 6–2, 6–3. Raul was a Mexican full of guile and speed who, although he had never won any major tournaments, played a very cunning match.

John's tennis received an additional booster when he teamed up with likeable and lively Australian, Wendy Turnbull, for mixed doubles. He suddenly started doing what he had been unable to in singles – win Grand Slam titles.

Wendy had left school at fifteen and worked in a bank in Brisbane before joining the tennis circuit. She shot to international stardom at the US Open in 1977 by beating Rosie Casals, Virginia Wade and Martina Navratilova to reach the final where she was runner-up to Chris. She had then concentrated on doubles and chalked up a distinguished record in Grand Slam events.

Wendy had known Chris and John for years through mutual Florida friend, Ana Leaird, and is one of Chris's closest friends on the circuit. It was Ana who asked Chris whether she had any ideas about a mixed doubles partner for Wendy, who wanted to team up with someone to play the French Open and Wimbledon. 'What about John?' Chris suggested, volunteering her husband's services.

'But aren't you two going to play together?' Ana queried. Chris confirmed that they weren't and so the successful Lloyd-Turnbull partnership began.

John and Wendy may have seemed an incongruous couple to some – the tall, quiet, smooth 'Pom' and the short, extrovert 'Aussie' – but they proved to be a highly complementary duo on court.

'We thought we'd be a good doubles team but we were better than we both had imagined,' Wendy laughed. Years before she had been nicknamed 'Rabbit' by Ilie Nastase's Romanian friend, Ion Tiriac, because of the speed with which she dived for, and returned, what looked like sure winners, and John also praises her reliable first serve and solid volleying. In turn, John's good crossing at the net intimidates the opposing woman, and his variety of shots keeps their opponents in a state of anxious guessing.

Their first tournament together, the French Open in May, started to show promising signs of being a success story after a few rounds. In the semi-finals they beat Americans Bruce Manson and Pam Teeguarden 6–7, 6–3, 6–1 for a place in the final, and John suddenly realized that he had a chance of a Grand Slam title.

Chris had pointed out to him how close he was to a major win: 'Even though it's not a singles title wouldn't it be nice to have your name on the championship roll!' Mixed doubles rank in importance after singles and doubles both in terms of prestige and prize money, but as John seemed unlikely ever to be in line for a singles title he didn't belittle being a mixed doubles victor.

In the final Wendy and John beat Brazilian couple Cassio Motta and Claudio Monteiro 6–2, 7–6 in a match which showed what a formidable mixed doubles partnership they had quickly become.

'I was nervous as hell but it was a great thrill when we won it and I was really proud. We played well and solidly – not great but we didn't have to. We were never in any doubt after the first four or five games that we'd win it,' John said.

It was a success which helped to compensate for Chris's loss to Andrea Jaeger in the semi-finals of the same tournament and John's defeat at the hands of lanky Frenchman Yannick Noah with a score of 7–5, 6–0, 6–3 in the third round of the singles. John had led Noah, the black Frenchman whom Arthur Ashe had discovered in the Cameroons, in the first set when he succumbed to the pressures of playing a star. Noah was a French idol who went on in that French Open to lose to Guillermo Vilas in the quarter-finals but who won the tournament in 1983, the first Frenchman to win it since Marcel Bernard in 1946.

'I didn't think I was good enough to beat Noah. I was giving him too much respect, playing the man instead of the ball,' John reflected and Noah's scintillating attacking tennis sent John down. However, his computer ranking jumped to no. 172 as a result of the points he collected in Paris.

He played powerfully in his next tournament – the Stella Artois, at Queen's Club, London, immediately before Wimbledon where he beat American Bruce Manson who was the sixteenth seed and ranked no. 46 in the world. John beat him 6–3, 7–6 and saved a set point in the tie-breaker before taking it 9–7. 'Lloyd on the way to revival', trumpeted the sports pages of the national dailies and John more than justified the wildcard he received straight into the Wimbledon draw.

There he met Russell Simpson of New Zealand, whom he had every chance of beating, and showed confident signs of doing so after a good first hour. He was two sets and two games to love up in the third when he lapsed back into his old way of losing when he was out in front: 'The old concentration went,' he later apologized, and Simpson went through to the second round, 3–6, 4–6, 7–6, 6–4, 6–4.

But there was another string to John's bow – the mixed doubles – and he and Wendy fought their way through to the finals beating Chris Johnstone and Pam Whytcross 5–7, 6–4, 6–2, which meant that both Lloyds found themselves in Wimbledon finals for the first time ever. Chris, who had won Wimbledon three times before and been runner up five times, was playing against Martina Navratilova in the women's singles. John and Wendy faced South African-born Kevin Curren and Texan Anne Smith in the mixed doubles, which offered John the momentous opportunity of becoming the first Englishman since Fred Perry forty-six years before to take a Wimbledon title.

Two victories that July weekend, which was the climax of one of the wettest and dreariest Wimbledons ever, would have been an excuse for the Lloyds to host a spectacular party – but it was not to be. Chris walked on to the Centre Court with niggling doubts about whether she could actually beat Martina, whose form on the way to the final had indicated the success of her comprehensive training schedule which had turned her into a formidable athlete.

Chris recovered from a disastrous first set, which Martina won 6–1 in only twenty-two minutes, to take the second 6–3. In the third she broke Martina's serve to lead 2–1 and Martina broke back to prevent Chris taking an unassailable 3–1 lead by attacking furiously. Chris was serving 15–0 in that game and later admitted she was suffering from lack of confidence.

'Even though I was up a break I didn't a hundred per cent believe I could really win that match. It showed right away when I was serving because I hit the balls in the middle of the court and Martina came in. Once I'd lost that game I felt I'd had my chances.'

Martina was buoyed up by an astonishing run of wins – only one loss in fifty-four matches – and the match was clinched by her serve and volley game to which Chris, as yet, had no answer. Martina defeated Chris 6–1, 3–6, 6–2 which meant she then had three-quarters of a Grand Slam.

More galling was John and Wendy's defeat with a score of 2–6, 6–3, 7–5, the only finals match that year to go three sets. 'We had our chances and let them slip away which made the defeat harder to accept,' Wendy described in her no-nonsense analysis.

John was particularly disappointed and every shot of the close third set is etched on his memory. He blamed the loss on his own lack of killer instinct. 'We were 2–0 in the third, up a break. We were always struggling on Wendy's serve and they were on Anne's. Kevin and I were holding ours pretty comfortably so whichever woman held her serve would win. Wendy was serving at 30–0, Anne hit a ball and I hit a volley, she returned it and I went across the net and hit an easy forehand volley. She had come running into the net and was standing five feet in front of me. I had to volley and I could have nailed the ball at her hard and knocked her out. Instead I just put it at her feet easily. She stuck out her racket, hit a lucky bucket lob over Wendy's head and they won that point. Kevin then hit a great shot and we were 30–all.'

That was the turning point of the match and it haunted John afterwards. 'I would have blasted the ball if I hadn't been returning it to a woman and had been a bit more ruthless. I was devastated at losing because it was my first Wimbledon final and I thought the chance might never come again.'

Wendy, Ana Leaird and Chris went out to console each other over dinner while John stayed at home watching a video, brooding gloomily over the defeat. He was still morose days later when Chris flew off to Australia to play in the Indoor Championships in Sydney and an exhibition match in Perth.

John was not only brooding about his defeat but also about the state of his marriage. He knew Chris was not happy – they missed each other less when they were apart, communication between them was spasmodic and focused on the trivia of their day-to-day lives rather than the problems of the real gulf that had grown between them.

It was during the summer when they were apart for weeks on end – talking only infrequently on the phone and then mostly about match results, circuit gossip and travel plans – that Chris struck up a close relationship with Adam Faith, a showbusiness entrepreneur who had been an international pop celebrity in the 1960s.

Ironically he was, if anything, John's friend to start with. The two men had met several years before when sharing the first class cabin of a flight to Los Angeles. Adam had told John he was a tennis fan and John, who has always been rather in awe of show business celebrities, had offered to get him tickets for a tournament. The offer had turned into a fairly regular favour and a casual friendship had grown. In time – with the provision of tickets for Wimbledon and the annual autumn women's tournament in Brighton, close to the Faiths's Sussex home – John naturally introduced Adam to Chris and his own parents.

Though no player himself, Adam gained something of a reputation as a tennis 'groupie'. He would often be seen around the players' tea-rooms during tournaments avidly listening to the chatter among professionals and generally joining in the camaraderie that exists between players, their entourages and officials. On several such occasions he had tea with the Lloyd parents, with whom he was as bright and sparkling in conversation as he was with everyone else.

He was a particular follower of the women's game. 'He was amusing, charming, witty, charismatic, certainly different from most of the men they meet every day on the circuit,' said one commentator who was around at the time.

People couldn't help but notice Adam; at the below-average height of about five feet four inches and in his forties he was conspicuous amongst the lean, long-legged young players. His casual, even scruffy attire of jeans and dirty sneakers – one tennis buff doesn't ever recall seeing him in a jacket – made him highly visible in the stands, too, particularly at Wimbledon where he looked a bit of an 'oddball' in comparison to the besuited, establishment members of the All England Club.

It was almost inevitable that Chris, miles away from home, should find him attractive. He was absorbing company and the two came slowly to talk more and more. He was much older than her; his experiences of life were so different; and he brought with him the eccentricity in mannerisms and dress of the world of show-biz. He frequently lapsed back into cockney, addressed everyone as 'love' regardless of their sex, yet drove a Rolls-Royce. For Chris, who is intelligent with an inquisitive mind and enjoys nothing more than challenging verbal exchanges on a range of topics (almost as if to make up for the years when her life was all tennis), Adam was a stimulating companion and his unconventional attributes were magnetic.

Looking back on it now John doesn't blame Adam or anyone else. 'You can't feel vindictive about it when you remember the state our marriage was in.'

As the circuit progressed around the world on its monotonous annual cycle, so the relationship, a contrast to loneliness and tedium for Chris, flourished, and so also the gossip started. Like all speculation it thrived on Adam flying to where Chris was (and John's absence) and on the couple's total refusal to confirm or deny an affair.

It is a reticence she has to this day, principally for John's sake. 'John and I made a pact not to discuss what went on with other people during this period and during our separation later,' she said.

Over the next few months she found in her growing friendship with Adam so much of the communication, warmth and stimulation that had disappeared from her marriage to John. For a while it thrived, but it could never really last. Tennis pressures, family pressures, press pressures and the fact that, in the final analysis, there were two marriages at stake finally brought it to a close.

All Chris says of the episode now is: 'When John and I announced our separation the opportunity presented itself for Adam and I to develop our relationship into something more permanent, but nothing of that sort materialized and we stopped seeing each other.

Adam wasn't the reason why John and I separated. If he had been, I would have been at his side the day after John and I made the announcement. And that thought never entered my mind. It was over.'

John said, 'Separation was the start of Chris and I getting back together,' and covers his hurt well, but he admitted, 'It took something like her friendship with Adam to stir us up and realize that we had severe problems with our marriage. But I said to Chris all the way through that even if we finished, Adam would not be the right person for her.'

For the remainder of 1982 John and Chris tried to bury their marital problems in order to support each other at the four Grand Slam events in which they were both competing. At the US Open in September Chris's 6–3, 6–1 victory over twenty-year-old Hana Mandlikova not only gave her her sixth US Open crown but also the first quarter of the much prized Grand Slam as well.

'I was in a kind of trance out there because I wanted to win so badly.'

Then, winning the Grand Slam entailed holding all four titles – Wimbledon, the French, US and Australian Opens – in the same season. The following year the International Tennis Federation altered the rules to cover holding all the titles at the same time, not necessarily in the same year. It is a feat which only a handful of 'greats' has ever achieved. Don Budge, the American player with the relentless backhand, was the first to win a Grand Slam in 1938. Australian Rod Laver won it as an amateur in 1962 and as a professional in 1969. Maureen Connolly was the first woman to achieve a Grand Slam in 1953, followed by Margaret Court in 1970.

Chris's stunning 6–3, 2–6, 6–3 victory over Martina Navratilova in the Australian Open at Kooyong in December gave her half a Grand Slam. The French the following June and Wimbledon a month later, if she could achieve them, would complete it.

Winning the Australian Open gave Chris tremendous pleasure and satisfaction: she had beaten the top seed and defending champion, more than avenged Martina's defeat of her in the same tournament twelve months previously and played her best ever tennis on grass.

Peggy Gossett, the Women's Tennis Association's media director, who is always at the court-side as players come off after shaking hands at the net, has noticed that normally after a match Chris doesn't say much. 'Win or lose, she generally takes a while for things to sink in unless something very dramatic has happened.' Her Kooyong win fell into that category, Peggy remembered. 'Chrissie heaved a big sigh of relief as if saying, "Boy, that was a tug of war," and she said, "This feels good." '

Chris became the sixth woman to win all four Grand Slam titles and this filled in what she described as 'the missing link' in her career. 'I would have hated to look back in ten years and see something was lacking in my record, especially as I did reach two Australian finals before and lost both in three sets,' she said after the match.

It was a triumphant tournament for Chris but a traumatic one for John who had also gone to Australia with hopes of doing well. He played Joe Meyers in the first round, an unknown American player whom he should have beaten. However, an attack of his old affliction – negativism – cost him the match. 'I remember Chris watching with Andrea Jaeger. I think I won the first set then I just gave it away and didn't try at all. I was playing rubbish. I felt embarrassed and just wanted to get off court and not face anybody. Chris waved at first to spur me on but the more she did that the more I thought "nah".'

After the game a disappointed Chris had to talk her devastated husband out of quitting tennis once more.

There was little time after John's match in which to enjoy Chris's magnificent victory. Following the prize-giving Chris went back to the hotel to collect her bags and then straight to Melbourne airport where she and John said a fraught and tearful farewell. John was facing more than a month alone in Australia, his marriage and his tennis both in tatters, while Chris returned to the United States.

While they were in Australia they had talked about the strain their marriage was under and, as Chris put it, 'the cloud hanging over us'. They had decided that as she was scheduled to play tournaments in America immediately after the Australian Open while John was planning to stay on to play in Sydney, Melbourne and then New Zealand, they would use those weeks apart to think about the future: should they attempt to get back together again, try a separation or call it a day and file for divorce?

Chris's hasty exit from Melbourne was to enable her to get in some tennis practice with Dennis Ralston before the Toyota Series Championship in New Jersey in mid-December.

Ironically, in the very tournament where Chris disposed of old enemy Tracy Austin – whom she had once feared she might never beat – 6–0, 6–0 in the semi-finals, Martina scored what would be the first of thirteen consecutive victories over Chris during two years until Chris beat her 6–2, 6–4 in Key Biscayne, Florida in January 1985. Martina defeated her 4–6, 6–1, 6–2 in the final, and seemed almost to go into another gear in the third set.

John Barrett wrote in the International Tennis Federation yearbook: 'The final set demonstrated clearly why Martina Navratilova has become a great player instead of merely a good one. With the world watching and waiting she rose magnificently to the challenge . . . These were the shots of a champion whose touch and confidence were riding high.'

Alone once again, John set about doing something constructive to improve his tennis, seeking help from a man eminently qualified to give it – Stan Nicholes, a former weightlifter turned physiotherapist and masseur whom John Newcombe had recommended. He had trained many top sports people including Herb Elliot, one of the world's greatest middle distance runners, Margaret Court and Australia's Davis Cup team.

Stan's empire is a small one-storey house in the Melbourne suburb of North Caulfield and it was there one hot Australian summer's day that John went.

'He asked me if I could help him because his game had gone to pot,' Stan recalled. 'I put him through a gym workout and was shocked and amazed to find that the strength in his shoulder muscles and his tennis strokes was less than a girl of thirteen. One of the exercises I gave him to test his shoulder muscles involved lifting a pair of 15-pound dumb-bells which he had difficulty in doing. A thirteen-year-old girl who was in the gym did the same exercise using 17½-pound dumb-bells, at which John realized how weak he was.

'He had an old shoulder injury which had never healed properly. He had never strengthened his shoulder and all the muscles in that area were wasted. He couldn't serve properly so had had to change his service action. The tricep muscle at the back of the arm, a muscle strongly involved in the tennis service as the arm is straightened, had atrophied and the deltoid muscles covering the shoulder joint were also very wasted. I'd seen similar injuries and knew that if he didn't do something about them himself he might need an operation. The shock of realizing just how weak his shoulder was showed John he was at the point of no return – if he didn't do something drastic then he would be finished as a tennis player. You cannot help athletes with an injury unless they want to be helped. John was crying out for help; he just needed the right sort.

Endless strenuous hours under Stan's supervision in the gym did wonders for John, strengthening him and fittening him immeasurably. It made him realize too what hard work was all about. Stan imbued John with his conviction that fitness and strength allow athletes to produce their top ability, and if they're fit they also enjoy the game more.

This intensive training was the beginning of the resurgence of John's game, but his unhappiness about his personal life continued, and he saw little hope of ironing out the problems in his marriage. When he'd completed his tournaments in Australia and New Zealand he flew to California to join his parents who were on their annual holiday at John and Chris's Rancho Mirage home, while Chris remained in Florida where she'd spent Christmas with her family under considerable parental pressure.

'That was one of the worst Christmases of my life. Things were strained because I hadn't really talked to my parents and they just didn't know what was going on, though they had been hearing rumours. Basically it was a lack of communication between us. I think my father was very hurt by it all. He and my mother loved John and thought I wasn't being very smart.'

Chris acknowledged that there had been certain times in her life when she had found it tough to live up to her parents' expectations, to live by the rules they'd laid down about morals and how to live, and this was one of them. 'We hadn't had anything like divorce in our family and I think the prospect was a shock to them.'

John telephoned Chris in Florida and asked whether her feelings had changed at all?

'No, they haven't'; I think we need a separation,' Chris replied.

'I don't want a separation, I think we'd better get a divorce,' he said.

She argued, 'A divorce is too final; we've been through too much together.'

John issued an ultimatum for the first time: to split up permanently or to get back together and make it work.

'That's when I thought about it and made up my mind to go back,' Chris remembered.

Ron Samuels acted as the go-between and, unbeknown to John, arranged for Chris to fly into Palm Springs from Florida while John and his parents were still holidaying there. John was talking to Mr and Mrs Lloyd by the pool across the road then walked into the house to find Chris in the lounge. As an outcome of that meeting, they both agreed to try harder.

However sincere that positive intention it turned out to have an only temporary effect and Chris soon felt that nothing was improving. 'We weren't getting any closer; we were like strangers, forcing our marriage to work.'

The next year, 1983, was characterized by a lot of time apart, a few long distance telephone calls and the odd week back together trying to patch things up. Chris remembered that they kept talking about separating then would put off making the decision. When it was convenient for one of them to make the break it wasn't for the other.

After the Palm Springs meeting John had to return to Australia to play Davis Cup against Australia in Adelaide, where he played the opening singles rubber against teenager Pat Cash.

John had made such a big impression on Stan Nicholes that as official masseur and conditioner for the Australian Davis Cup team Stan felt divided loyalties about the Lloyd and Cash match. He said to Neale Fraser, the Australian captain, 'John Lloyd has done a great job on his shoulder and I'm anxious to see how he goes.' But Fraser said he thought that John's best tennis was behind him.

Stan remembers bristling at that remark: 'It made me even more determined than ever to make sure John pushed himself. When he played 'Cashy' it was the only time in thirty-five years of being with the Davis Cup that I didn't care whether Australia lost.'

However, Australia won the match and although John was defeated by the seventeen-year-old Pat Cash he put up a tremendous fight. The score of the close and thrilling final was 5–7, 7–5, 6–3, 1–6, 7–5, after which John earned himself unanimous praise including some generous comments from British captain, Paul Hutchins. 'I thought it was a great effort from John considering a few weeks ago he was pretty unfit and unmotivated. He's picked himself up off the floor and proved he can play a great match. I'm delighted for him.'

John carried on working hard although his improved form was insufficient to avoid a disappointment in the opening round of the first Grand Slam event of the year – the French Open in Paris in May – where he was defeated by American Eric Fromm, 3–6, 7–6, 6–2, 6–3.

In the same tournament Chris went through to the final where she met Yugoslavian Mimi Jausovec whom – on a hot and humid Paris afternoon – she utterly outclassed to win her fifth French title, securing the third leg of the Grand Slam. The 6–1, 6–2 score indicates that Jausovec never got into the match.

Chris's track record over her opponent, Kathy Jordan, whom she was to meet in the third round at Wimbledon on 24 June, was also impressive. They had played five times before and Chris had won handsomely on every occasion without so much as the loss of a set. Chris's path through the draw to success in the final, to become the third woman in tennis history to complete the Grand Slam, looked assured.

The evening before the match, the Lloyds's cook, Jenny Scally, prepared a dinner of barbecued steak, green salad, baked potatoes, fresh fruit salad and cream for Chris and John, Mrs Evert, Chris's brother John with whom she was competing in the mixed doubles, Ron Samuels and his girlfriend, Kathy and a couple of other friends at the Lloyds's Kingston house. She said goodnight and left at about 11.30.

The following grey afternoon she watched Chris's match on television with her mother in their New Malden flat and was shocked to see a drawn, pale and ill-looking Chris lose the first set 6–1. Television commentators speculated what could be wrong as the upset of the three-times champion, five-times runner-up who had never lost before the semi-final at Wimbledon in eleven years, looked increasingly likely.

Jenny's heart sank as she heard the commentator say, 'Mrs Evert Lloyd really isn't very well; I wonder what she's eaten?' 'I just sat there thinking that I knew exactly what she had eaten. I felt awful,' remembered Jenny. She mentally ran through her 'safety' rules for the Lloyds, precautions meant to eliminate any risk of food poisoning or upset stomachs, both of which Chris and John have been frequent victims of: fresh fish but no shellfish; nothing frozen. She wondered what could have been the culprit.

When Chris lost the tense tie-breaker in the second set Jenny prepared to drive to Wimbledon to find out what was wrong, but just then the telephone went. It was Chris, who told Jenny, 'Never mind what happened; I just wanted you to know it wasn't anything I ate, to put your mind at ease. I can assure you it wasn't anything to do with food.'

Chris made that call after hurriedly leaving the post-match press conference which she stoically attended, looking a ghostly white, to be sick again before John drove her home to bed.

Niacin, of the vitamin B complex, was the culprit. Chris had taken a tablet the previous evening after dinner. Kathy Smith, a Californian fitness expert and nutritionist, was staying in Chris and John's house during Wimbledon; she had taken niacin for years, building up her dosage from the normal starting amount of 50 milligrams to 500-milligram capsules. Chris and Kathy's bottles of vitamin and mineral pills had been in separate groups in the kitchen, but whoever had cleaned up the kitchen had stood all the bottles together. Chris swallowed her normal dose of iron and vitamin C then looked at Kathy's bottles and saw niacin. Recognizing it as a standard ingredient of practically every packet of cereal, she didn't even consider it might be dangerous or read the dosages, and took a pill.

For someone like Chris who has a very low tolerance of drugs and even reacts to aspirin and alcohol, 500 milligrams of niacin was a considerable overdose. Less than an hour afterwards she asked John whether he thought she looked funny. He commented that her skin was very blotchy and she looked flushed and asked her what she'd taken.

He smelt the pineapple juice which she'd had a glass of to see if it was off then read the instructions on the niacin bottle which said if Chris's symptoms occurred drink plenty of water. He quickly told Chris to do that, but it didn't help and her heart began racing.

'I was running round the house, up and down the stairs as if I was on drugs. I thought I was going to have a heart attack because the palpitations were so bad,' remembered Chris.

John called the doctor who came and gave her an injection but only after she'd been terribly sick. It wasn't until the early hours of the morning that she fell into a fitful and exhausted sleep, having been very ill.

As soon as the referee's office at Wimbledon opened at nine o'clock John telephoned Alan Mills and asked if Chris's match could be postponed for a day because she'd been ill, and was told that it couldn't because the match was in the order of play. Once a player's name has been inserted in the order of play (the schedule of matches which is drawn up the previous evening) then he or she can only default or play the match, and cannot request a postponement.

John woke Chris who was feeling very weak. She said that she felt as if she had been through a war but wasn't going to default the match. After a breakfast of tea and dry toast she went to Wimbledon still thinking that she could win.

'I felt too weak to practise. I just lay on the locker room massage table resting and conserving my energy, and Dennis Ralston gave me some glucose tablets.'

John, who was praying for rain, watched the match sitting between Mrs Evert and Dennis Ralston, under leaden skies on court 1. The whole party looked strained and anxious as Chris lost the first set. Ron Samuels was sitting in front of John and remembered, 'It was a nightmare; we were all sitting there like robots. Knowing her body language I could see how hard she was struggling.'

Kathy Jordan was playing fine tennis, way above her usual standard, but Chris, even though she had so much less power in her strokes than usual, established a 4–1 lead in the second set. John was panicking but he thought she might just be able to win.

Unfortunately Chris couldn't hold on to that advantage against Kathy's fiery serves, volleys and huge forehands, and although Chris went on to lead 5–3, Kathy levelled at 6–all to force a tie-breaker. After an hour and thirty minutes, Kathy (who lists reading fiction among her hobbies) must have seen the far-fetched coming true when she took the tie-breaker 7–2 and the match with an ace on first match point.

John remembered, 'I was utterly devastated, and was wondering what must Chris be feeling after all she'd gone through. She'd been so close to a Grand Slam and it was being taken away from her without a hundred per cent chance.'

Chris was a generous loser and made no excuses at the post-match press conference. 'I met Kathy on a day when she played great lawn tennis; she had an on-day, I had an off-day. I wouldn't have walked on court if I hadn't thought I was fit, or that I didn't have a chance to win.'

Chris went home to bed, trying to ignore the press who were out in force in the road outside and kept ringing the doorbell to ask to take photographs of her in bed. A kind of numbness settled over the household.

Ron said, 'I think we were all in shock for a couple of days. Chris felt disappointed for us because our trip to England had been a present from her. She'd paid for everything – first-class air-fares, a car and driver at the airport – and had invited us to stay with them. She was concerned about how we felt, almost as if she'd let us down.'

Chris still had to play in the mixed doubles with her younger brother, John, and in the women's doubles partnering Billie Jean King. Chris and John were defeated in the opening round by John Fitzgerald of Australia and American, Betsy Nagelsen. She and Billie Jean were seeded eighth and got through to the third round before losing to Kathy Jordan and Mimi Jausovec, 5–7, 6–4, 6–3.

Unaccustomed to having time on her hands during Wimbledon, Chris visited the Tower of London and jogged in Richmond Park which was within easy reach of their Kingston house. They had bought it early in 1982 because John's Wimbledon bachelor flat was too small. Named Willow Cottage because of the tree in the front garden, it is an attractive, modest, traditionally English, four-bedroomed house with a walled garden, situated in the stockbroker belt.

John and Wendy took the Lloyd name into the mixed doubles final for the second year running. John had lost to Craig Miller of Australia 6–1, 6–7, 2–6, 6–3, 6–1 in the opening round of the singles, but he and Wendy played well all the way to the semi-finals where they defeated Fred Stolle and Pam Shriver 6–4, 4–6, 6–3 for their place in the final against Billie Jean King and Steve Denton. Kevin Curren and Anne Smith weren't defending their title because after the French Open in June Anne had decided to exchange tennis for retirement in Dallas, Texas and raising horses.

On 3 July John had his second chance to become the first Englishman to win a Wimbledon title since Fred Perry. Having lost the final the previous year but won the French Open two years in succession, John and Wendy were determined not to be runners-up at Wimbledon a second time.

The match was a nail-biting struggle, and an enormous and excited crowd saw mixed doubles being played at its best. There was only one break of service in the whole match – Billie Jean King's in the last game. Two tie-breakers decided the first two sets – Billie Jean and Steve won the first and John and Wendy the second.

Mrs King served at 6–5 down in the third set and Wendy described the match from that point: 'At 30–all John said to me, "OK, move your feet on this return, just move your feet." I did, hit a good return and John crossed and hit it for a winner. On the next serve, match point, John hit a great return with topspin and Billie let it go. "Leave it," she shouted to Denton, and it landed in. The crowd went berserk, and John and I jumped in the air and hugged each other.'

The entire crowd, led by Chris, rose to its feet with a patriotic roar to give its victors a rousing standing ovation. At the press conference, Chris warm-heartedly said, 'John has been upstaging me all week and I'm delighted.'

A celebration was called for so after the Champions' Ball the Lloyds's party made for Tramp, arriving just as John remembered that it's shut on Sundays, so it was back to the Lloyds's house and – as it was John's day – the video, but no horror, just endless re-runs of the tape of the doubles victory. Until the early hours of the morning John slow motioned his and Wendy's most brilliant shots and freeze-framed Ron, Kathy and Chris in the stands until they all knew the whole match backwards.

Since that Wimbledon triumph Wendy has also played doubles with Chris and once had the crowd in uncontrollable laughter when, after they'd won the Virginia Slims Championship in Los Angeles in October 1984, she compared John and Chris as partners: 'I prefer playing with John because he's a better player and he has better legs,' Wendy mischievously confided into the microphone. 'He's also got a better bum but Chris won't let me check that out!'

John fled from the stands in embarrassment and Chris was giggling helplessly, down on bended knee on court. 'Please will you ask me to play with you again,' she'd begged Wendy, pretending to be in awe of the mixed doubles champion which had prompted the Australian to consider which Lloyd she preferred.

Originally it had been John's wish that he and Chris should wait until after Wimbledon before separating, but when the time came they put it off. They discussed it again before Flushing Meadow and the US Open in September, but John felt that the horrendous publicity which would inevitably accompany a separation announcement would be detrimental to both their performances.

'I was trying to make a comeback and I thought it would be tough to have the spotlight turned on us. I was in rather a fragile state and I didn't want anything else to make me worse.'

John's comeback efforts paid dividends in the 1983 US Open and he played inspired tennis to beat Jose Higueras from Spain, ranked tenth in the world, in a memorable second-round match which lasted over two hours in blazing hot conditions. It was a 6–3, 6–4, 7–5 triumph: many people judged it to be the best tennis John had played since he defeated Roscoe Tanner at Wimbledon in 1977, and certainly the Lloyd resolve, determination and tactics couldn't be faulted.

John then beat Terry Moor 6–3, 5–7, 2–6, 6–0, 6–1, to reach the last sixteen before being beaten by Mark Dickson 6–7, 7–6, 6–0, 7–6.

John explained that it was the realization that it was now or never which had prompted the spurt his fans and followers had waited so long to see. Now he had to sustain it.

While John was proving that he was once again capable of beating players ranked in the top ten in the world, Chris was finding how hard it was going to be to find a way of defeating Martina, the world's no. 1, without new weapons in her arsenal to combat her opponent's superb athleticism and awesome serve and volley game.

In a final held in the 93-degree heat, Martina won 6–1, 6–3 to gain her first US Open title in eleven attempts, giving Chris the worst pounding she'd suffered in any Grand Slam final. It was Martina's tenth consecutive victory.

To John and Wendy Turnbull's disappointment they couldn't add the US Open's mixed doubles championship to their Wimbledon title, but they did reach the semi-finals before American top seeds Ferdi Taygan and Barbara Potter beat them 7–6, 6–3.

It was a measure of the firm bond between John and Chris that although their marriage was heading irretrievably towards a break-up – and possibly a permanent one – they discussed whether John would benefit from investing $30,000 in a coach. Chris remembered her advice: 'If you feel it will help your game and motivation it will be a good investment.'

The discrepancy in their earnings had not caused any problems until then. 'I've never been one to worry about finances or Chris making more money than me,' said John. 'In those three disastrous years when I made no prize-money whatsoever I'd fly first class if I was with Chris and we'd stay in nice hotels although I was actually losing money.'

Suddenly John began to have reservations. 'I thought, how can I justify paying $5,000 to Warren Bosworth, the man who strings my rackets and $30,000 to a coach when I'm not really earning anything? If I was by myself living on what I was earning I couldn't afford to pay that much. I talked it over with Chris and she was marvellous about it and said straightaway, "Don't even hesitate."'

So John joined Australian coach Bob Brett and his squad, which included Harold Solomon and the American brothers Sammy and Tony Giammalva, determined to work hard, raise his singles rankings and make up for the years in the wilderness.

Chris went to Japan with Andrea Jaeger, Martina and Hungarian Andrea Temesvari to play a four-woman exhibition match on the way to the Australian Open in Melbourne the following month.

In Tokyo she decided to withdraw from Kooyong, unable to defend her title because of a recurrence of a foot complaint, plantar fasciatis. It had started when she sprained the arch of her foot on a seven-mile jog in Richmond Park with Kathy Smith, when she'd had so much spare time after her Wimbledon defeat by Kathy Jordan. She decided to return to London rather than going to support John in Australia.

'I don't like it one bit that you're going to London,' he told her on the phone, hurt and angry, but Chris flew there anyway.

John played well in the Open and beat big-serving Steve Denton 7–6, 6–2, 6–3 in the third round before losing to Johan Kriek 6–3, 6–3, 7–6. This match showed John how moody Johan could be, which John remembered nine months later in the 1984 US Open, to his benefit.

Chris telephoned John in Melbourne from London: 'I think we should meet in Los Angeles; we have a lot to talk about,' she began. 'There's nothing to say,' John fired back.

'I could tell by the tone of his voice that he was saying it was all over,' Chris recalled, and she persuaded him to meet her at Ron and Kathy's in Los Angeles where the procrastination ended, they decided to part and Chris flew to Florida to spend Christmas with her family while John remained with Ron and Kathy in California.

Looking back on 1983 afterwards, Chris reflected what a wasted year it had been because they had continually put off solving their marriage problems. 'There was so much indecision; it makes me think we were too sensitive to what other people would think,' she said. 'We couldn't make up our minds what we wanted to do, but John and I are like that; we never do things without a lot of thought. By the end of the year we had realized that separation was inevitable, whereas before we'd kept saying, "Let's forget it for a couple of weeks and try again."'

When the split had come, they had parted without acrimony. 'We'd still look at each other and smile, and never felt bitter. That was a tribute to John, not to me,' said Chris.

John and Wendy Turnbull win the Wimbledon mixed doubles in 1984 for the second year running. *Tommy Hindley*

A victorious salute from Chris after defeating Martina in the 1985 French Open final. *Tommy Hindley*

Hotel life: tea, coffee, vitamins and minerals for breakfast. *John Hawkeye Hawks*

(Right) Back to normality again.

(Opposite) It's the Wimbledon plate which really counts. Chris after her third Wimbledon victory in 1981. *Tommy Hindley*

(Overleaf) Happy birthday, John! The brand new BMW was his thirtieth birthday present from Chris. *Art Seitz*

CHAPTER NINE

1984
Separation

Fans, the tennis world and the Lloyds's friends learned that their golden couple had parted when Bob Kain, Corporate Vice-President of IMG (their agents), issued a short statement on their behalf on 28 January, 1984. He telephoned the major wire services from his Cleveland office and told them that John and Chris had agreed on a trial separation but remained the best of friends.

Chris felt ambivalent about going public with the announcement: on one hand she regretted the negative impact it would have on their public image, one of the prices she has to pay for having been on a public pedestal since she was sixteen; but as a woman she felt she had the right to be normal and human.

'I thought I was just being real mixed up and that I was no different from anyone else. Just because I was a champion tennis player it didn't mean I couldn't have problems in other areas.'

Chris was staying with Ron and Kathy in Los Angeles when Kain's statement hit the radio and television bulletins and appeared in newspapers, so she was protected from door-stopping journalists anxious for any titbits of gossip simply because they couldn't find her.

John, who was playing in an indoor tournament in Memphis,

Tennessee, had no such protection and found himself so hassled by reporters at his hotel and the courts that he enlisted the help of player and friend Drew Gitlin as a 'minder' to keep them at bay.

Neither Chris nor John spoke to the media hordes who stalked them because they had agreed not to give any exclusive interviews telling their side of the break-up story. They behaved, as they did throughout the six-month separation, with dignity, style and a loyal consideration for one another's feelings.

Such was the public esteem and respect in which the Lloyds were held in England, that British newspapers treated their separation with sadness rather than the sensationalism and cynicism with which they can splash news of rifts in celebrities' marriages.

John and Chris telephoned one another each evening in the days following the separation announcement to keep in touch and talk about the publicity until John decided that they ought to observe the literal meaning of separation.

'The sixth night in a row that we talked on the phone,' Chris remembered, 'John said, "We're separated now; we really shouldn't ring every night," so I said, "Well we'll call every two weeks." "Yes, OK," he said, "but no more than that because we're apart now and we should really get on and live our own lives and see what we really want. Even if you decide you want to come back to me I'm not definitely sure that I would want to make it work." '

Separation was a risk for both of them and John's resolution and decisiveness surprised her but she realized his firmness was what was needed and she agreed with him.

Chris flew to the east coast of the United States to compete in the Virginia Slims Championships in Madison Square Garden, New York where she appeared with a new body-waved layered hair style and mid-size graphite Wilson racket. Both suited her: the hair with its lift and curl was pretty and very flattering and the racket a success. 'I loved it; it felt easier to play with and I had more reach.'

She toughed out an exciting match against Kathy Jordan, beating her 7–5, 4–6, 6–3 in the first round, and said afterwards, 'I was very pleased because I hung in there when others would have given up.'

There was no denying that although the separation had been largely at her instigation, the trauma of it affected her concentration, confidence and her game. 'My tennis level dropped five to ten per cent during the six months we were apart. I was more easily distracted and as much as I wanted to bury myself in my tennis it was always secondary to my marriage problems.'

It was exactly the reverse of how Chris had reacted after her engagement to Jimmy Connors had been broken off. Then she had exorcized the hurt and unhappiness she felt by playing more aggressively and immersing herself in her game. This time it was John who did that and put the effort he hadn't been able to find for five years into resurrecting his singles game.

'It was Jimmy then who had made the decision and I was on the receiving end,' said Chris. 'This time I knew that John loved me, but the decision was in my hands and I was mixed up.'

'In a sense the tragedy of John's marriage falling apart was the making of him,' John Barrett said. 'Here was the necessity to re-establish himself; here was something really brutal happening and not many bad things had happened to John before. Everyone had been very kind to him, he had so many friends and I think the shock got through to him. It was almost a therapy to throw himself into hard work again and get away from the worry of the separation.'

John practised hard and consistently with Bob Brett and although he was fitter, having stuck to Stan Nicholes's fitness programme, Bob's routine was an eye-opener, illustrating to him the real meaning of hard work and how he'd skipped it for the past few years.

'Straightaway we started playing three or four hours a day on court and physically I wasn't used to it; it took my body time to adjust. I hadn't practised under those intense conditions. I wasn't hard enough and I couldn't keep my concentration. I'd miss a ball and throw my racket in the fence. When I looked back over my career I realized that I'd never worked professionally. Although I'd never been a drinker and had always kept myself in shape – I'd been sensible and was probably fitter than fifty per cent of the guys on the circuit – I've only really learned how to prepare properly in the last year with Bob.'

When John and Chris had finalized their separation in Los Angeles the previous December they had known that they were both going to be seen with new dates and discussed how best to handle it. The ground rules they drew up were not to go out with other tennis players (that would have been too close to home, Chris said), to be discreet about their affairs, and to incur the minimum publicity so one didn't open the paper and see the other with someone else.

They knew any photographs of them in some trendy nightspot with a new partner would be plastered all over the tabloids and gossip columns with an 'other woman' caption under a blonde of John's or 'the new man in Chris's life' under any male she was spotted with.

John said, 'In the States, someone was offered $10,000 to take a picture of Chris in a compromising situation with another man.'

The arrangement was that if either of them saw flashbulbs popping and lenses aimed in their direction while they were out with someone else they would telephone and warn the other about what might be in the following day's papers. This worked quite satisfactorily, as Chris remembers. 'As it turned out there were never any pictures and there were no big scandals. It was funny because I said to John that a couple of the guys I went out with thought I still had feelings for him and he said, "That's exactly the same with me. A couple of the girls thought I was still in love with you." '

'I think we were both so sensitive to each other's feelings, and John was always on my mind. I went out with other people who I liked being with a lot but didn't find anyone I wanted to spend the rest of my life with.'

As the separation wore on the communication between them lessened as they developed their own lives. 'We talked on the phone every two or three weeks,' Chris said, 'but there was a strain.' 'What have you been doing?' the natural question in any casual conversation, is a difficult one to hedge around when you don't really want to divulge to your spouse that you've been going out with someone else.

They only seriously talked about a final separation once when they made a preliminary visit to a Florida divorce lawyer and accountant in the spring. They discussed divorce proceedings, how the money could be split up and their business commitments disentangled, if it came to that. It had been John's idea: 'It was one more way of showing I was serious,' he said. 'I telephoned Chris and said that I thought we should go and see a lawyer and talk it over, and she agreed.'

Throughout the spring and early summer of 1984 both Lloyds were preoccupied with their thoughts about whether to get back together again or split up permanently.

Chris spent a lot of time alone mulling over what she wanted to do with her future and it was three months before she dated anyone else. She likened the decision-making process to 1980 and her sabbatical when she didn't know whether to retire or make a comeback.

'In both cases I didn't wake up one morning and realize I had the answer; it was more gradual. I knew that I had to look at the future as a whole and not at one week or one year at a time.'

John's keenness for her to retire particularly worried her. 'He said, "If we get back together again I won't want you to go on playing after this year. A family is very important to me and I'd like you to stop and have kids." That turned me off because I didn't want anyone putting pressure on me,' Chris said.

John tried to prepare himself for either a divorce or a reconciliation. 'I always knew I wanted her back but I was trying to put up a barrier because in some ways I was trying to make myself accept the fact that it was over. Deep down I wanted to get back together but I didn't want to show Chris that because I didn't want to get badly hurt again. I'd already accepted that we were going to get divorced last December, then we'd separated which raised the possibility we might get back together, but I didn't want to get devastated a second time. I put up an emotional protective barrier in case in a few weeks' time Chris said, "I want to get a divorce."'

Chris vacillated about reconciliation and whether it was the right move. 'Some days I felt very independent and thought, "I've got to start a new life," but other days I thought, "I'm being really stupid; I've got this great guy, shouldn't I go back to him?"'

With this question mark hanging over the future of their marriage neither John nor Chris was looking for a spouse replacement amongst their lovers. Chris went out with other men because she didn't want to feel she hadn't looked around and dated enough; John, through a distaste for the monastic life, lapsed into his old bachelor ways and his liking for leggy models.

Hard work on his tennis started to pay dividends for John and in the opening round of the French Open in Paris in June he played a great match to beat British no. 1 Colin Dowdeswell with a score of 6–4, 6–1, 2–6, 6–4. On the same day Chris suffered a shock defeat at the hands of seventeen-year-old Bulgarian Manuela Maleeva in the finals of the very wet Italian Open in Perugia.

Chris avenged that defeat within a week in the Open in Paris and then went on to notch up her fiftieth win in the French tournament with a victory over blonde Canadian teenager, Carling Bassett.

Chris spent the fortnight of the French Open with Kathy Smith to keep her company, plus Dennis Ralston and Adam Faith's ex-secretary Melanie Green. She had become a friend of Chris's and spent six weeks with her in France and Britain as an aide and companion.

John and Chris watched each other's matches – John lost in the second round to Jimmy Connors 6–4, 6–1, 6–4 while Chris proceeded through the quarter- and semi-finals, where she beat the left-handed American Camilla Benjamin, to play Martina in the final.

'I thought that I'd have a good crack at her in Paris because clay has been my best surface in the past.' But those hopes of victory were turned into a bad loss when Martina, playing at her best, beat Chris 6–3, 6–1 for the first time on clay. It was a profitable win for Martina as she collected the million-dollar bonus put up by the International Tennis Federation for the third woman ever to win the Grand Slam.

'That was the best she played against me all year,' commented Chris. 'She played real clay-court tennis and moved unbelievably well. I think she played better tennis in the first half of that year than in the second.'

It was Martina's eleventh consecutive victory over Chris and did nothing to reassure Chris that she was closing the gap on her opponent who played awesome and daunting tennis.

John flew back to Paris for the day to support Chris to honour a deal they had made to watch each other whenever they reached a final. He was also more hopeful than he'd been in recent months that he and Chris would eventually get back together. He knew Chris loathed being alone both in her private life and on the tennis circuit. She had always travelled with her mother, a girlfriend or her husband and not having anyone permanent to act as an aide in her professional life and a companion in her private life exacerbated the loneliness of the circuit intolerably.

During Paris Chris made the first move towards reconciliation. From her luxury hotel suite in the Hilton, close to the Eiffel Tower, where she has stayed for every French Open, she called John and they talked about their five months' separation.

'I've made up my mind that I'd like to give it a try,' she told John who, wary of a return to all the indecision of the previous year, wanted a more definite, positive commitment. In reply to her offer he added his own condition: 'I don't want to give it a try, I want you either to come back or not.'

They spent the night together in Chris's suite, John dodging photographers as he arrived and left. 'We were petrified that someone would see us,' John recalled as once again, just like he had at the US Open in New York in 1978 before they were married, he found himself sneaking cloak and dagger style in and out of luxury hotels to see Chris.

Chris suggested then that they get back together but John disagreed. 'No, the time isn't right; let's wait until after Wimbledon when we'll have peace and quiet and people will leave us alone.'

During Wimbledon John stayed in his and Chris's Kingston home, which he shared with Drew Gitlin and other player friends, while Chris rented a town-house in Wimbledon close to the All England Club and had her mother to stay. She had little privacy because she was beseiged by press who were casting around for indications of the state of her marriage. They were also hounding Martina Navratilova, who had rented a house just across the road in Wimbledon, with questions about her relationship with Texan housewife, Judy Nelson. This prompted both the world's no. 1 and no. 2 players to speak out strongly about media intrusions into their private lives.

Chris felt that while she was happy to attend the post-match press conferences and answer questions about her games, tennis and the tournament, she resented the personal questions from the non-tennis general reporters who also crowded into the interview rooms.

Chris beat Swedish Carina Karlsson 6–2, 6–2 in the quarter-finals and Hana Mandlikova 6–1, 6–2, in the semis to face top seed Martina who was eager for her fifth Wimbledon title in the final. It was the fourth Navratilova-Lloyd final at Wimbledon in seven years, and a memorable one for women in other ways: Georgina Clark, an Oxfordshire mother of five who was the only woman in Britain to hold an A1 umpire's grading, was in the chair, the first woman to umpire a final. It was also the 100th anniversary of women competing in the tournament.

Chris started playing well and ran up an encouraging 3–0 lead, then a tentative approach to the match developed in the back of her mind and Martina went into another gear. 'She started to rise to the occasion,' Chris remembered. Martina took the first set with a tie-breaker and the second 6–2, making her the first woman since Billie Jean King in 1966 to 1968 to win Wimbledon three consecutive times.

It was Chris's twelfth consecutive loss to Martina but a much less serious defeat than in Paris. Despite the psychological hold Martina had built up over her, Chris now thought that one day she would triumph over the no. 1 in the world.

'A lot of people tell me that when I go out and play her the pressure is on her, that I've got nothing to lose. It's not as if I've been no. 20 all my life – being a champion and having been no. 1 I know that I've got to the top before and that it's within my reach. When you've been close to a competitor and have won Grand Slam events you know you really should beat her if you're playing your best.'

John had a very satisfying Wimbledon. He got through to the third round, equalling his best-ever performance in the tournament, and earned compliments for the controlled, mature tennis he played to defeat American Greg Holmes. His hopes of further advancement were ended by another American, Scott Davis, who defeated him in straight sets 6–4, 6–4, 7–6.

Chris watched John and Wendy Turnbull's successful defence of their mixed doubles title with a victory over Steve Denton and Kathy Jordan, 7–5, 7–5, which was a cause for great celebration in the Lloyd household. She also went to the barbecue which John hosted for players, family and friends but she didn't go on with him to the champions' dinner at the Savoy in order to avoid the publicity and speculation their arriving together would have fuelled.

During Wimbledon Chris and John made no definite plans about when and where they would get back together again. They were both still occasionally going out with other dates but being doubly careful while the tournament was on to ensure their relationships remained private.

Chris raised the topic of reconciliation again. 'Remember what I said at the French,' she reminded John. 'I'd like to make a go of our marriage.'

'I would too,' he said, and a little over five months after the issue of the separation announcement they decided they preferred life together rather than going it alone, and neither of them had found anyone else.

Another factor influenced Chris; she is not the sort of person to walk away from anything unless she has given it one hundred per cent. At the back of her mind she knew that marriage involved give and take: 'I realized that John had given more and I had taken more,' she said.

On the Monday after Wimbledon Melanie Green drove Chris back to her and John's home in Kingston. In her mind Chris ran through the six months she and John had spent apart, and how their marriage was going to be different in the future.

'I had re-thought what I really wanted for my future, where I was going. I believed that the way John had handled everything showed his true character. I decided to make a commitment to him, and I think he realized that whatever commitment you make in life it entails a risk.

'The new rules were that we weren't going to spend much time apart. We were going to look at our schedules and be together each week if possible, and grow together instead of apart. John had more purpose in life, he had made a commitment to his tennis and had a better self-image. He had grown up and he realized why I had lost respect for him.'

They had also reached a compromise on the issue of having a family, agreeing that they would both like children one day but not putting a definite time limit on it.

Her suitcases back home in the hall, there was the momentary awkwardness of reconciliation as they sat down on the couch together. 'I felt kind of funny for the first couple of minutes. But in my heart I felt determined to make it work, and if you put a lot of effort into something it works more easily. I didn't want to say too much. I wanted to go back to being a wife, and to be with John, but I didn't want to make too many promises because I thought actions speak louder than words.'

CHAPTER TEN

1984
Martina in her Sights

It was like an oven on the courts but Chris was used to that. She had hit her first tennis balls twenty-five years earlier on the public courts near her home, in that same punishing humidity and exhausting heat of a Florida July.

Her father was, and still is, the pro at those Holiday Park courts in Fort Lauderdale and, over the years, the tennis regulars there have got used to his all-time champion daughter practising in their midst. What made this practice session the week after Wimbledon 1984 different was that Chris was hitting with John, the husband from whom she had been publicly separated for the past six months.

The Lloyds had slipped out of London and flown home to Florida in an elaborate cloak and dagger operation, aided by their cook and housekeeper, Jenny Scally. Jenny had once worked for British Airways and knew how to avoid the newspaper stringers and photographers who stalk Terminal Three at Heathrow Airport. Chris and John wanted a few days' peace before the world knew they were back together and pestered them for the 'marriage mended' story.

However, that day, as they neared the end of a hot session, they looked up from their game to see a photographer pointing his camera in their direction.

He approached John and Chris who were furious at having their privacy invaded, but reluctantly came to a professional agreement with him. 'You're not wearing the clothes you endorse,' he started. 'And we're sweaty,' they countered. 'So why don't you come over to the house for fifteen minutes and take a decent set of pictures?' compromised the Lloyds. He did just that and the publication of the resulting photographs served as a reconciliation announcement.

A few weeks later, in August, Chris and John adjourned to their apartment at Amelia Island in Florida for a breather in between the European tournaments and the US Open at Flushing Meadow the first two weeks in September.

Bob Brett, John's coach, was with them and they both worked out with him. Then Chris and John stayed for a few days with Ron and Kathy in Los Angeles where Chris bought John his thirtieth birthday present. It was a couple of weeks early – his official birthday wasn't until 27 August when they would be at the US Open.

'Why don't you wait until the day?' John queried as Chris and he piled into Ron's Rolls Royce for the purchase of the extremely generous gift. 'I can't,' Chris reasoned, 'because we'll be in New York and what I want to give you is here.'

'I suspected it was something to do with video equipment,' John remembered, since he had been raving about a special new piece of electronic gadgetry. In fact it turned out to be a very swish metallic grey BMW 633. John was thrilled: 'The only car I've ever really loved the look of!'

One of Chris's characteristics is doing things in an extra-special way so the smart birthday car arrived with a personalized number plate: FLOSS 1, after John's early nickname, Flossie, because of his flowing locks.

Before the start of the US Open the couple went their separate ways to play. John went to the ATP Championships in Cincinnati and Chris flew to Montreal to compete in the Canadian Open where she beat the six-foot-tall, nineteen-year-old Czech, Helena Sukova (who would shoot to fame in the Australian Open four months later) 6–1, 6–2 in the semi-finals; and blonde Stanford

University student and fellow Wightman Cup team mate, Alycia Moulton, 6–2, 7–6 in the final. She then flew straight to New York that evening to join John for the US Open.

For the first time they had taken an apartment in the St Moritz Hotel on Central Park and Fifth Avenue and flown Jenny Scally over from Kingston to cater for and look after them.

In the tournament John played some of his best ever tennis. To everyone's amazement – perhaps even his own – he beat Peter Fleming, Johan Kriek and Henrik Sundstrom before losing to Jimmy Connors in the quarter-finals. He then reverted to playing his usual support role to Chris, but with a new pride and self-respect from having done so well himself.

'There's Chris's husband, John, in the stands,' the CBS commentators said as the TV cameras focused on John in his trendy sunglasses, but for once he wasn't merely a spouse. 'What a great tournament he's had; super tennis,' they said.

He was watching Chris in her ninth final against the adversary she had met in the other two 1984 Grand Slam finals in Paris and Wimbledon – Martina Navratilova, whose third American final this was. Chris had progressed smoothly through to the last round, beating Sylvia Hanika of West Germany 6–2, 6–3 in the quarter-finals and Canadian Carling Bassett 6–2, 6–2 in the semis.

Her opponent now had beaten her twelve consecutive times since December 1982 and on the way to this game had beaten fellow Czech Helena Sukova in the quarter-finals and Australian Wendy Turnbull in the semis.

It was nearly dusk when the match started and the lights had already been turned on so the players could get accustomed to the change from daylight to artificial light. The atmosphere was super-charged as Chris and Martina walked on court. The crowd sensed that they were in for a great match between the world's no. 1 and no. 2.

In the first set Martina played ragged, impatient tennis and made a high percentage of unforced errors. At two games-all in the first set Virginia Wade, who was commentating for CBS, praised Chris: 'She's moving as well as I've ever seen her move.'

175

Martina broke Chris's serve to lead 4–3 but Chris broke back to level at 4-all, taking advantage of the fact that Martina was still playing sloppily. Chris led 5–4 with Martina serving to save the set. At deuce, a double fault gave Chris the advantage and set point. A perfectly calculated and deftly executed volley into the open court won her the first set 6–4 in thirty-six minutes.

Seeing the shot was a winner, Chris turned, bent her arms and clenched her fists as the crowd erupted in appreciation. 'I have never heard such an ovation from the crowd; it was deafening. It was great and I got choked up. I think everybody – including me – anticipated that there could be a big upset.'

Martina broke Chris's serve early in the second set for a 2–1 lead and Chris faced a crucial turning point when she had an opportunity to level at 5–all. Martina was serving for the set 5–4 and was down 15–40.

'That was a huge game,' Chris recalled, but she didn't come in on an easy second serve of Martina's which made it 30–40 and then returned a good first serve into the net and it was deuce. Martina went on to take the set 6–4.

'I had two opportunities to win those vital points but didn't take advantage of them and my spirits started to sink. Martina rarely offers such chances and she'd given me not one but two. It would have been a very close match if I had won one of those points and got to 5–all.

'Martina's great when she's winning easily because she gets into full gear, but in close matches she gets nervous. A score of 5–all might have got to her a little bit.'

As at Wimbledon, where Chris had built up a 3–0 lead in the first set, she had started out well but hadn't kept it up. 'I had definitely let down in the second set,' she said remorsefully afterwards.

In the third set Martina started to get into her stride and broke Chris's serve to lead 2–1. She broke it again to take the US Open title for the second consecutive year with a final score of 4–6, 6–4, 6–4. It was the sixty-first match between the two players since their first meeting in 1973 and Martina's win tipped the balance in her favour – 31 victories to Chris's 30.

Chris was completely shattered and felt a loser's sense of total isolation as she sat down in her court-side chair, only just managing to fight back tears.

'I felt I had had my big chance for the first win against her in two years and I'd blown it. I realized then, too late, how desperately I had wanted it. I hadn't even felt like that at Wimbledon. When I'd played Tracy Austin at Flushing Meadow in 1980 and had my chance I'd felt the same way.

'During the prize-giving ceremony it was a struggle and Martina didn't say anything to comfort me – she was so happy that she'd won. The crowd was clapping really hard for me; I think they appreciated the effort I'd made. I said to myself, "OK, stay cool and calm." The TV cameras were on me during the presentation and I was crushed. For a minute I thought, "Don't show how you feel;" then I thought, "Damn it. Why shouldn't I?"

'My dad told me later than the TV commentators said they'd never seen Chris looking so disappointed. It was true – that's how I felt. I was tired of pretending everything was all right.'

Chris reflected too on the colossal support which the crowd had shown her as the underdog and how it had unnerved, annoyed and irritated Martina. 'Martina feels very threatened by the fact that whenever we play the crowd is always on my side. For so many years when I was no. 1 the crowd was against me yet I had to put up with it. Now she was no. 1 she had sour-grapes about it which annoyed me a little bit. I would much rather be no. 1 and have the crowd cheer for my opponent because there's nothing personal in the cheering – it's just that they want to see a close match.'

Chris, who wanted to be alone in defeat, spent fifteen minutes in the referee's court-side office before going into the press conference and then along to the first-floor locker room to pack up her gear – a routine a winner can cruise through but a dismal exercise for a dejected loser. 'When you lose, everything's a drag,' Chris said wryly.

The long drive back into New York with John gave her a chance to think more lucidly and analytically about the match. She was concerned, just as she had been when Tracy Austin had beaten her in the 1979 Italian Open, that these two defeats were rare instances of her not being able to pull the stops out and win a close match.

'Ninety-nine per cent of the time when I really wanted to win a match and was in a tight situation, I was able to do it. Somehow I'd be able to dig deep down into my reserves and get that extra something. This time I'd dug deep and it just wasn't there. It was one of the few times that this had happened. I actually felt very human; I didn't feel as though I was invincible, although over the years I'd been classified as a real tough cookie competitor.'

Ron Samuels, who was with the Lloyds in New York, remembers that Chris was encouraged by the closeness of the final, realizing that she had what it takes to beat Martina and that it was only a question of time.

Nevertheless Chris's first victory over Martina after this was rather hollow. It was an exhibition match for the Martina Youth Foundation at Rancho Bernardo, California, three days later. The usual uptightness which plagued Chris whenever she played Martina was absent.

'I went into it loose, aggressive and a little angry at having lost to her at Flushing Meadow, so I returned well. She was distracted; it was a night match and she was having trouble with the lights. Chris described it as a 'bitter-sweet victory', and wondered why she hadn't done it in the US Open, when it counted. 'It meant something to me personally but it didn't mean anything to anyone else.'

However, it did give Chris much more confidence; Martina was firmly in her sights and she would keep gunning until she got that first win. Her problem was the difficulty of changing her game after twenty-three years as a baseliner. Ingrid Bentzer summed it up in her inimitable way: 'Chris never came into the net – unless it was to shake hands at the end of the match!'

Seasoned veteran Judy Dalton spelt out how hard the task was that Chris had set herself. 'Chrissie has been brought up so much as a baseliner that it's foreign for her to go to the net. It's very hard to change: Borg tried but couldn't do it and gave up. At least to Chris's credit she's still trying.

Chris said: 'I'm working on my first serve to make it a little bit harder with more depth and trying to rob Martina of the chance to use the net. The last couple of times I've tried that I've come closest to beating her, so now it's a case of trying to put a volley and bigger serve into my game. Getting motivation and being hungry is important, too.'

Chris's next shot at Martina would be at the Australian Open in December, three months away, so there was time for a break before their autumn tournament commitments and that last Grand Slam event of the year downunder.

John and Chris took off for a second honeymoon in Palm Springs and one which was rather more successful than the first. Chris hadn't seen her home for a year and a half because during their marriage problems and separation she'd allowed John and his family to have the use of it. Back there again she re-discovered all the attractions which had initially so impressed her about the desert resort.

'I just couldn't believe how much I enjoyed it – the mountains, nature, the crisp air and the clean living. John and I spent three days by ourselves then Kathy and Ron came down. We went to the gym in the mornings or on hikes in the Indian reservations; then we played some mixed doubles in the afternoons for fun. We'd go out to eat and I cooked on a couple of nights. Once we had Ray Moore and his wife over; it was great fun, a very healthy kind of week.'

Rested and refreshed, Chris's next commitment was the fifty-sixth Wightman Cup at London's Royal Albert Hall where she captained the US team of Alycia Moulton, Gretchen Rush, Barbara Potter and Sharon Walsh to a five rubbers-to-two victory over Great Britain which was represented by Virginia Wade, Jo Durie, Annabel Croft, Anne Hobbs and Amanda Brown.

Chris defeated Anne Hobbs in the opening singles on 1 November, but Annabel Croft levelled at 1–all with a stupendous match against Alycia Moulton which she won 6–1, 5–7, 6–4 and had the Albert Hall on its feet cheering.

John played escort, impeccably dressed in a grey designer-label suit, although he discovered that being the VIP husband of a superstar captain of the American team didn't mean an automatic court-side seat. When officials couldn't find enough seats together the Lloyd party was despatched to an upper box – 'right up in the clouds', John complained.

Chris dropped retirement hints, saying that as the Wightman Cup is played alternate years in Great Britain and the United States her doubles victory in partnership with Alycia Moulton over Virginia Wade and Amanda Brown might be her last appearance in Britain.

Abiding by the new Lloyd reconciliation rules to spend the minimum time apart, Chris stayed on in London after the Wightman Cup to support John who was competing in the Benson and Hedges tournament at Wembley in early November. On the first morning of John's tournament Chris was up very early to make an appearance on breakfast television. Despite the unsociable hour (which is far from her favourite time of the day) she looked chic and was witty, articulate and polished. Tennis for Chris and John is like anyone else's job; they are interested in other things and don't only talk about the game. In the players' lounge at Wembley, for example, pre-match conversation ranged from the Australian elections to the causes of cot deaths, news at the time.

She watched two of John's matches. He won his opening one against American John Sadri, then lost the next one against Peter Fleming, who he had beaten in the US Open two months before but who proved too tough an adversary on this occasion and defeated John 6–3, 6–2.

It was a draining match to watch and afterwards Chris joked – although there was a hint of truth in it – 'I could never be a tennis wife, it's too tough,' as she made her way back to the players' lounge, signing autographs and photos of both John and herself as she went.

In the packed lounge she flipped through a paperback by Shirley MacLaine and chatted to Mr and Mrs Lloyd as they waited for John to appear from the dressing-room. When he did she instantly turned her attention to her disappointed husband for a private moment, oblivious to the hubbub around them.

'I didn't play too well, did I?' murmured a rather deflated John, his fingers touching Chris's. With a mixture of the tenderness of a wife and the constructive advice of a top tennis player she whispered her encouragement: 'You beat Peter when it counted, in the US Open, which was the bigger tournament.' Quickly moving positively to the future she said, 'For the Australian Open you've got to work on your serve.'

'Peter played ninety-five per cent of his potential; John played about seventy-five,' she said, rehashing the match later on and proud that John had competed to the end and not given up. 'It was much closer than the 6–3, 6–2 score shows,' she emphasized.

Before the match she'd found time to discover a new clothes shop and had added several Italian designer-label outfits to her wardrobe. John had recommended this particular designer since he already owned several of his suits. She invested in some striking leather jackets as well as trouser and sweater ensembles, and was particularly thrilled that for the first time John had picked out a few garments for her. Previously he had always just murmured compliments about a new hairstyle, make-up or outfit.

'He doesn't usually have any confidence about selecting women's clothes, but he picked out two or three sweaters and said that he really loved them. I tried them on and bought them. I was excited because he's never bought me any clothes before, though I've always said "Go ahead, take a chance; if I don't like them I can always take them back."'

Chris knows what she looks good in and that her best points are her straight back and small waist. 'As far as summer is concerned, I've always stuck with whites. I love black for evenings, and sequins if they're not too gaudy. I prefer things that fit at the waist because I'm short and otherwise my body looks boxy.'

She had also spent half a morning with builders planning extensive renovations to their Kingston home. She planned a luxurious new master bedroom and bathroom en suite on the first floor, and conversion of the double garage, which they don't use because neither drives in London, into a fitness complex with gym, shower and sauna. All of this added up to a considerable show of confidence in the Lloyds' future together for those who were still wondering whether they were really reconciled permanently.

Once Chris's West End shopping spree was over and John was out of Wembley, it was time for another move in their nomadic lives. They packed up new clothes, old clothes and tennis gear in preparation for the journey to Melbourne for the Australian Open. Packing is a chore which even with their type of existence the Lloyds haven't yet got down to a fine art.

'I'm pathetic, I really am,' said Chris. 'I'm OK with my tennis stuff – I pack six skirts, six blouses, ten pairs of socks, six pairs of tennis panties, three sweaters and two tracksuits, but I'm really bad on regular clothes. We have seven bags between us; two are all rackets then I have three full of clothes and John has two. It's not really that much when you think that often it's for two months. If I've just been shopping I'll usually take the new clothes even if they're not practical to travel with or suitable for the weather.'

This explains why, some weeks later in Sydney, packing to fly for a week's holiday up to tropical Hamilton Island on Queensland's Barrier Reef – where the mode of dress is a bikini and swimming trunks – Chris was folding into her suitcase her two new leather jackets and a couple of winter tweed outfits. They were her purchases from that shopping expedition which were still with her.

On the other hand John seemed to have evolved the method of packing only dirty clothes on the grounds that this meant he could just throw them in his bag instead of folding them up!

Not only do they dislike packing for a journey, but also neither of them are enthusiastic about the actual flying. Despite the amount she has to do, Chris loathes it and gets afraid sometimes because she feels she's not in control. She rarely sleeps, doesn't drink and only picks at a brown bread roll or a modest portion of cheese and fruit. John doesn't like being in the air either, and they both look distinctly uneasy at the first sign of turbulence.

Chris and John arrived in Melbourne nearly two weeks before the start of the Open to put in some strenuous training at Stan Nicholes's gym. It had been John's idea that Chris should join him as part of her masterplan to beat Martina Navratilova and so halt her run of defeats by the world's no. 1, at the same time as taking her second Australian title and sixteenth Grand Slam win. She had won a Grand Slam title every year for the past eleven years and she needed this one to keep her impressive record intact.

Stan was worried about the 'little dump' he's got. 'I thought Chris would be a spoilt champion but I found out the reverse; she's a terrific person and as we started to train we got to know and respect each other.'

So it was to Stan's homely gym in suburban North Caulfield rather than to some smart, air-conditioned fitness emporium that Chris went daily. She worked with characteristic dedication which won her praise from Stan who has trained some of the world's best and toughest competitors. 'This woman is like cold steel the way she trains in the gym. She's absolutely determined, and just grits her teeth. When I demonstrated one exercise I said to her, "If it's hard only do five; if it's comfortable do ten." How many did she do? Twelve.'

Stan also tried her with an exercise designed to improve her spring to help her leap for smashes. It entailed holding a dumb-bell in each hand and jumping on and off a 20-inch-high stool. Chris couldn't manage the dumb-bells at first so Stan started her on it without them. After a while, he gave her a pair of light 5-pounders but Chris didn't stop there and within a fortnight she was hopping on and off the stool with a 12½-pound dumb-bell in each hand.

John worked out conscientiously, too, with Bob Brett and two new members of their squad – twenty-one-year-old Stuart Bale from Middlesex and American Tom Cain.

Chris practised daily with Stewart, as well as with Bob and John, because as a left-hander he was invaluable preparation for playing the anticipated final against Martina.

John was seeded no. 10 in the Open, the first time he'd been seeded in a Grand Slam event for more years than he cared to remember. He was looking for a good tournament to consolidate his result at Flushing Meadow and was full of hope because he had reached the last sixteen at Kooyong the previous year.

He drew his Wembley opponent of a few years before, John Sadri, who managed to find the winning form which had eluded him in London and defeated John 6–4, 3–6, 7–6, 6–3. John was very disappointed but consoled himself that he was back at no. 24 in the world rankings – equal to his best ever when he was twenty-three years old.

Once out of the Open he kept up his practice schedule with Bob, Stewart and Tom because it wasn't his last tournament of the year. He planned to play a series in Australia before going on to New Zealand in the New Year.

He practised with Chris too and found time to solve some of the other tiny crises which cropped up, such as on the day she arrived at Kooyong for the match which was to give her her 1000th singles victory without any tennis panties.

She sent John to enlist the help of Peggy Gossett, the Women's Tennis Association's Director of Public Relations. Peggy was typing furiously in the press-room when John burst in with the urgent message that Chris, who was due on court imminently, was dressed in everything minus her knickers.

Peggy sped up to the pro boutique by the main gate and got two pairs – one the wrong size, the other the wrong colour.

'I went running (it's a good thing I jog every morning) and got two more pairs so Chris had four. She narrowed it down to a choice of two – either yellow with dark blue stitching or plain white because she was wearing a yellow, blue and white dress.'

With a minute to go before the match, it was Pam Shriver who acted as catalyst and forced Chris to stop dithering about which pair to wear. 'Chris, there comes a time in your life where you have to make a decision and never look back.' So Chris stepped into her new A$5.25 yellow panties and made for the court.

Her opponent was French teenager Pascale Paradis, whom she had never played nor even seen play before. This fact, combined with the panties drama and the hype which had surrounded the match because it could be her thousandth win, did nothing for Chris's nerves and she lost the second set tiebreaker.

The Chief of Protocol, Ted Tinling, had organized a mammoth blossom-pink cake with a thousand candles on it. He had chosen the colour on purpose because it appealed to his sense of the romantic and he thought Chris was a romantic person, too.

But Chris's none too promising performance and loss of the

first set put the celebrations at risk. 'What do we do if she loses?' Brian Tobin, President of the Lawn Tennis Association of Australia, asked Ted. The incorrigible Ted replied, 'Well, you just forget the whole thing,' and hatched his contingency revenge plan.

'I was prepared to tell Virginia Wade that she could eat candles for a week because Virginia coaches Paradis so it would have been her fault if Chris lost.'

Miss Wade had a lucky escape from this diet of wax when her protégé couldn't sustain her fighting performance and Chris won the third set. The cake presentation was made and the thousand candles lit to comments from Chris about how relieved she was that it wasn't a birthday cake!

However, the flames suddenly began to leap perilously close to the roof of the LTA's marquee. Chris tried to blow them out but merely fanned them, at which a few guests started to edge towards the exits, until eventually a waiter achieved with a wet tea-towel what Chris's huffing and puffing couldn't. Ted wouldn't hear a word of criticism of the near inferno. 'People get very nervous; it never crossed my mind there was any problem at all. It looked very effective because the candles didn't melt so there was no mess – a neat inferno.'

If John and Peggy had solved the tennis panties crisis and an astute waiter averted the fire, it was Chris who played heroine when the lift in the Regent Hotel broke down with the two Lloyds and three other guests – one man and two girls – in it. She pushed the alarm button to announce they were stuck while the girls, who were slightly drunk, could only giggle and the man threatened to sue everyone in sight. The couple had been on their way to a launch party for the new book *What They Don't Teach You at Harvard Business School*, written by Mark McCormack, the head of IMG, their agents. John got claustrophobic and lay down on the floor while trying to soothe Chris who feared that they might suddenly plunge down thirty floors. It was to the considerable relief of all the passengers when the lift edged slowly upwards and the doors opened.

Chris's next victory was over her and John's doubles partner, Wendy Turnbull, in the semi-finals. In the press-room afterwards she was only asked two questions about the match and fourteen about her proposed tactics against Martina in the final. The only other question raised a titter: 'Chris, just in case, what's your record against the other semi-finalist, Helena Sukova?' The build-up for the projected Lloyd/Navratilova clash in the final was in full gear.

In fact, the nineteen-year-old 6ft 2in-tall Helena pulled off one of the most phenomenal upsets of the year by defeating the world's no. 1, 1–6, 6–3, 7–5. It was Martina's first defeat in seventy-five matches and only her second this year – the first had been at the hands of another Czech, Hana Mandlikova, back in January.

Ironically, Helena's mother, Vera Sukova, who was a Wimbledon finalist in 1962, had been one of Martina's early coaches when she had been on the Czech junior team.

When Martina took the first set 6–1, it looked as though it was going to be one of her merciless victories in quick straight sets. Earlier in the week, seventeen-year-old Kathy Rinaldi had taken a first set off Martina – only the eighth she had conceded all year – and was made to pay for it by Martina who won the next twelve out of thirteen games.

Helena was different and fought back to win the second set which had spectators excitedly converging on the Centre Court hoping for great things from the underdog. She didn't disappoint them, winning the match on the sixth match point!

It was a remarkable accomplishment and sent John and Chris – who had missed the match – off to track down a video of it so they could study the new girl who'd suddenly replaced the one she'd been gearing up to challenge for months.

Chris had played Helena five times before – most recently in the Canadian Open in August – and had never lost to her, so her chances of capturing a 1984 Grand Slam title had rocketed.

The video of the match was only of limited use to Chris because Helena's tactics against a right-handed baseliner were going to be different to the way she had played to beat Martina's left-handed serve and volley game. Nevertheless, John thought that watching it enabled Chris to pick up some of Helena's patterns – when she hit her passing shots down the line and when cross-court, where she served in each court most of the time and how much she had improved since Chris had last played her three months before.

The couple didn't spend all evening discussing tactics because Chris doesn't like to get wound up for a match too early. Instead they had a room service supper and relaxed in front of the television.

After very changeable weather all tournament the day of the final dawned with perfect blue skies. Chris got up at about 9.15 – nearly four hours before the match – and breakfasted an hour later on easily digestible carbohydrates. She practised with John and Bob who told her how well she was hitting the ball. The next time John saw her was just before the match, for a chat to psych her up and encourage her, outside the locker room.

'She said, "I'm very nervous," and I said, "That's good because it means you're really eager for the match." I told her, "You've got to think of Helena's position; it's her first Grand Slam final," impressing on her that Helena would be even more nervous. She was very concerned about Helena being on form because she had played well against Martina.'

He watched with Bob Brett and Stan Nicholes and their wives, his pre-match nerves turning to genuine anxiety when Helena took the first set by winning the tie-breaker 7–4. What worried him particularly was that Chris was struggling, not moving well and playing far below her best. 'I said to Bob, "This is getting dangerous. Maybe Helena's suddenly going to think she can win this match, whereas before she hadn't considered she had a chance." Chris wasn't playing that well and looked as though she was trying unbelievably hard but just couldn't get going. Bob was sure that she'd get one break and be all right from then on.'

John's fears proved unfounded and Bob was right: Chris won the second set and never again looked in danger of any sort. Although it hadn't been a great and memorable match it was a mission accomplished – a Grand Slam title.

While the dignitaries assembled on court with the cups and cheques and the ballgirls lined up for the presentation Chris chatted to Peggy Gossett by the umpire's chair. She reminded Chris that it was her sixteenth Grand Slam win. 'Sixteen, that sounds good,' repeated Chris with approval, but there were no wild displays of euphoria from her on court, and it took the usual amount of time for the victory to sink in.

She did give John a winning smile though. 'I gave her a wave back at the presentation and Bob, his wife Claudia, Stan and his wife Lynne, all met just by the locker room and gave her a little hug and said "Well done." She was a bit disappointed because she'd wanted to put on a great show because we were watching, but Bob and Stan said straight away: "Look, you came through; it was a tough match." She ended on the best shot of the match – a beautiful cross-court forehand.'

Chris had a massage and then with her usual devotion to duty first sat down to discuss with Peggy Gossett some of the business and policies of the Women's Tennis Association which Chris as President would have to deal with in New York.

John, meanwhile, kerb-crawled around suburban Melbourne in a tournament courtesy car trying to remember the location of two video shops so he could return an armful of tapes he'd borrowed. Debating whether to hire more horror for that evening, he resisted because he realized that it really ought to be Chris's occasion.

In their suite Chris relaxed. 'Betty Grable – what a dramatic entrance,' she joked as she hammed up coming through the sliding door between the bedroom and sitting-room. She had been on the phone organizing a group of friends to go out to dinner with.

She was in several minds about the win: pleased with the victory, but slightly disappointed that she hadn't played as great a game as she would have liked, and there was a bit of an anti-climax feeling that it hadn't been Martina on the other side of the net.

'I'm disappointed in a way that I wasn't the one to beat her. She's been vulnerable now for a few months and has been having some close matches with the other girls. The first thing she said to me when she came off court after she'd lost to Sukova was, "Well, I'm not giving you a chance to beat me," and she almost sounded relieved. I really don't think she wanted to lose to me; I think she'd prefer to lose to other people.'

Although Martina's run of thirteen consecutive wins over Chris would extend into 1985, Chris now clearly scented victory having worked and worked to close the gap between the no. 1 and no. 2.

It was an obstacle which had, at times during the past two years, appeared insurmountable.

But the rivalry has had its uses too. Mr Evert said, 'It would be interesting to speculate what it would be like if there was no Martina Navratilova. Would Chris be as dominating? Would she be as eager? Maybe if she was no. 1 she wouldn't be working as hard. In some ways perhaps it's all been a blessing in disguise.'

Stan Nicholes, after forty years of watching athletes come and go, couldn't help but admire her unbending determination not to remain no. 2 in the world but to strive until she reached the top by playing better and being fitter than she had ever been.

'Some athletes will train fanatically till they reach the top then it saddens me because they seem to be satisfied. But even with her thousand wins Chris still wants help to improve her game, which pleases me.'

Chris earned her mother's admiration too. 'She's a real champion because as good as she is she still feels she can improve.'

Chris described the source of this endless motivation, and the differences between her rivalry with Martina and that between her and Tracy Austin nearly five years before.

'Tracy and I had the same styles and I felt I was just up against a wall the whole time – because playing her was like playing myself. Martina and I have different styles and I feel she gives me a target. I can just concentrate on perfecting my game more, and working on the tactics which will defeat her. I don't think about how well she's playing; I merely do a few things better.

'Lately I have come close to beating Martina so I don't feel it's a fruitless effort, but with Tracy when she beat me, she really killed me. Martina and I are closer in age – she's a year and a half younger – so it's not as humiliating as it was with a sixteen-year-old kid. Martina and I have had such a great rivalry for ten years.'

The Lloyds had planned to fly up to Sydney on Saturday evening after the Open final where John was competing in the New South Wales' Men's Open which started two days later. Chris had decided to sacrifice spending both her thirtieth birthday and Christmas at home in Fort Lauderdale to remain in Australia with John. However, an airline dispute stranded them in Melbourne until the following morning.

It was a good excuse for an impromptu celebration and with a party of friends which included Wendy Turnbull and Peggy Gossett they went out for dinner at Vlado's, a popular restaurant famous for its steaks.

After the meal and back in the lobby of the Regent Hotel they ran into Martina and her friend, Texan Judy Nelson, Martina's coach, Mike Estep, and his wife, who'd all also just come in from dinner and invited the Lloyds to join them in the bar for a nightcap.

Chris and John differed as to whether to accept the invitation. John doesn't like to socialize and tried to excuse them by saying they had to pack. Chris was keener to accept and thought that she deserved the relaxation of a drink with friends. The woman who had been champion of the centre court less than twelve hours before now faced a conflict of interests: she was a victor wanting to unwind and modestly toast her victory, versus the wife and partner of a player who was getting keyed up for his next competition.

'I thought, "John has a tournament next week," then "Well, he could play on Wednesday so this can't hurt him." I said, "Come on John."' 'All right, just one drink,' he conceded, and they all adjourned to the bar.

CHAPTER ELEVEN

1985 and Beyond

Chris had waited for two years to see a scoreboard which recorded a 6–2, 6–4 victory for her over Martina Navratilova. When the win finally came it was a triumph of Chris's willpower after thirteen consecutive defeats at the hands of one of her greatest rivals.

Helena Sukova, with her surprise upset of Martina in the Australian Open, had deprived Chris of her chance to end 1984 with the desired win, but she'd finally accomplished it at their first tournament of 1985 – in the Virginia Slims Championship at Key Biscayne, Florida.

Chris found it merely 'satisfying' rather than a cause for hysterical celebration. 'I wasn't jumping up and down crying like I was when I beat Tracy Austin in the finals of the 1980 US Open. It was a more mature win – a gratifying achievement. People had started to wonder whether I would ever beat her again and doubts were beginning to creep into my mind, too.'

The public's fears about Chris's return to the very top were realized two weeks later in the Lipton International Players' Championship at Delray Beach, Florida when Martina demonstrated that she intended to do her best to ensure that Chris didn't beat her again this year. She came back strongly in the final to win with a score of 6–2, 6–4.

Nevertheless, that first win put 1985 in a new light as far as Chris was concerned, and she started to look forward to another twelve months of duels with Martina. 'It made me more eager to play her. Martina and I will probably meet eight or nine times this year, and now I'm really looking forward to those matches as challenges instead of dreading them. Martina isn't as invincible as she was a year ago,' Chris said in the aftermath of victory.

Key Biscayne punctured the Navratilova invincibility but it was Chris's dramatic defeat of Martina in the final of the French Open in June which was the truly glorious victory.

That win brought her even more than her sixth French championship and seventeenth Grand Slam title; it made her no. 1 in the world again, the exalted position she'd challenged Martina for for three years. Chris's 6–3, 6–7, 7–5 victory was a closely fought 2 hour and 53 minute battle, a roller-coaster of a match which could tantalisingly have gone either way.

Chris's see-sawing fortunes frayed her husband's nerves. 'It all depended on whether Chris really believed in herself. She won the first set then had so many chances in the second but she'd get ahead, establish control, and then start playing negatively, waiting for Martina to make a mistake rather than going in and winning the point as she'd been doing in the first set.

'When she lost the tie-breaker in the second I thought she was finished. I turned to Dennis Ralston and said, "She's blown it." I was worried because I thought to myself that if she loses this match she'll retire because she'll never have a better chance to beat Martina and she'll know it too.'

Chris drilled a two-handed backhand pass down the line to take the third set 7–5 and the match and prove John's fears unfounded. Minutes later, a breathless and overwhelmed champion clutching the trophy, she thanked her husband and coach for their contributions to her memorable win.

Afterwards, there was no time to indulge in fancy champagne celebrations: the Lloyds dashed from court to hotel to airport and caught a London-bound flight with only seconds to spare. The reason for their hasty exit from Paris, at John's instigation, was two-fold: he was anxious to grab every hour of practice on grass he could in preparation for Queen's and Wimbledon and, as a sporting buff, keen to see the boxing event of the year in London that night starring Irishman Barry McGuigan. So, the new French champion – no boxing fan herself – 'celebrated' her triumph with a TV dinner while John settled down in their Kingston home to watch his second sporting encounter of the day.

A few days later Chris enjoyed belated congratulations and toasts with a small group of people, which included her younger sister Clare who was over to play in the Wimbledon qualifying rounds, brother John and close friends, in Tramp, the West End discotheque where she and John had had their first date.

'I'd been waiting for that win at a big tournament for a long time,' Chris said, recalling how much the victory had meant. 'I'd had a lot of losses against Martina at major tournaments. During the French final I was playing well then she'd catch up but I didn't get down on myself so the mental part pleased me.

'The physical side was gratifying too because I didn't get tired which showed that all the hours of running and working out had really helped me.'

Ironically, during the first week of the French Open Chris had suffered such strong retirement pangs that for a few days she was almost tempted to finish her tennis career then and there.

'I wasn't playing well, I wasn't playing my best matches. It was hard for me to get psyched up and I was having tough contests against girls who normally I'd been beating pretty easily.

'Although I'd had the Key Biscayne win over Martina, I'd followed it with losses to Hana Mandlikova in Oakland, California, in February; to Kathy Jordan in New York in March and Zina Garrison in Florida in April. I talked with John and Dennis about retiring but then the next week I went out and played some of my best tennis ever and won the tournament.'

The thrill of that victory banished all retirement thoughts from her mind. 'Winning is such a great feeling that it makes you want to go on playing forever,' she said.

Realistically though, Chris appreciates that she is in the twilight of her career, and it is a tribute to her championship mettle that she is remaining competitive, working harder, and is fitter and playing better than ever before. She has won approaching 150 titles even though she's getting older, and today faces a crop of talented youngsters in the game of women's tennis which has greatly increased in depth. One of the most punishing parts now is that, unlike the early days of her career when only the semis and the finals were tough matches, every round is potentially very taxing.

Chris celebrated her thirtieth birthday on 21 December, 1984 – a milestone in a professional athlete's life and a landmark in a woman's. 'Age has never scared me,' she said. 'The only thing which does is that my tunnel vision isn't as strong as it used to be. I don't have the motivation and that worries me. Physically, however, I know that even if I wake up and I'm stiff or hurting a little bit, it may take longer to warm up but I can work my way out of that. You can still be a great athlete at forty-five.'

Chris takes heart from the fact that some of her greatest predecessors in tennis were still coming to their prime at her age: 'The great champions of our era – Billie Jean King, Margaret Court, Virginia Wade, Evonne Cawley – all peaked in their early thirties and I think that's very interesting. They all, like me, started playing at a young age and stunned the tennis world, but won Wimbledon at the age of about thirty. That's when mentally and physically everything came together in their game; they matured and they understood more what it's all about.

'The reason I'm still playing at thirty is because I feel deep inside that although it's going to be harder work for me I can still improve. That's really what keeps me going. If in the last couple of years I'd had a real downfall and had dropped from no. 2 to no. 3 and the next year slipped down to no. 5, then I would have started to think about continuing. But as it is I'm head and shoulders above anybody else, except for Martina.

'She is still the player to beat in women's tennis, but it's nice for us other women to know that she's not dominating any more.'

In 1985, Chris and Martina met six times; Chris won two of their encounters and Martina four, including the finals of both Wimbledon and the Australian Open – both grass surfaces for which her game is tailor-made and proved supreme.

John, too, during that year, at his own level, competed against several of the top players in the world and produced some of his best-ever tennis. He was especially satisfied when he took John McEnroe to a third set tie-breaker in the quarter finals of a Grand Prix tournament in San Francisco in September.

'To have come within two points of beating a man whom I consider to be one of the greatest players of all time was an honour, and I felt very proud to be out on court.' He was warmly congratulated on his performance by McEnroe, who won 6–1, 6–7, 7–6.

John started the year with cause to be pleased; he was no. 1 in the official British rankings for the first time since he'd featured on the list in 1973 and he was ranked 37th in the world – the only British player in the top one hundred.

He was both realistic and cautious about his ambitions. He knew well that his advancing years – 32 in August 1986 – and the growing competitiveness of the men's game, in which hungry, talented young players fight it out on the satellite circuit for every precious ATP computer point, threatened the revival of his fortunes, despite his belief that, like so many British players in the past, he too would play his best tennis late in life.

He has made strides, and has tanked matches far less often, showing a new-found professionalism and determination for which he can thank Bob Brett's creed: 'You haven't lost a match until you've been beaten.'

John was passionately keen to play well in the singles at Wimbledon. 'The best I've ever done there is win two rounds, which in ten years of trying is not great. I would like to play the best tennis I'm capable of and peak at Wimbledon and also win the mixed doubles with Wendy for the third time.'

'I think I'll know instinctively when to retire,' Chris said. She doesn't expect to be still playing on the Centre Court when she's thirty-eight – as Billie Jean King was – but she isn't necessarily looking at 1985's Wimbledon or US Open as her last. 'I'm not putting the lid on anything. The bottom line is, "Do I want to pay the price? Do I want to go on working as hard as I have? And when do I want to start a family?"'

Although she has won everything except the Grand Slam, she is adamant that she won't retire until she's satisfied that she has maximized every last bit of her potential.

'I feel I haven't yet had the most out of my body as an athlete. I've been a great tennis champion but I haven't been a great athlete, and I'm just trying to get all the positive aspects out of myself physically before I stop.

'But at the same time as I want to get the best out of my body, I have to remember that mentally I can't keep going with the same intensity; I've probably gone on a lot longer than anyone else in the history of the game: twelve years as a pro, no real slumps, and I've been in the top three my whole life. I feel that mentally time is running out but physically I'm in the best shape I've ever been.

'When the time comes I could go one of two routes: off the court completely and say, "That's it, I'm never going to compete in another tournament in my life," or I could slowly get out of the game and say, "This year I'm going to really concentrate on my tennis; next year I'm only going to play exhibitions and capitalize on the money." I don't know how I'm going to do it, I really don't.'

Even though Chris has won at least one Grand Slam title every year since 1974, her one final ambition is to win Wimbledon for the fourth time. 'If that happened,' said John, 'I think Chris would retire the next day with the biggest smile on her face she has ever had. That would be a real fairytale.'

John explained why motivation is such an essential commodity in Chris's game: 'She has to be really fired up and keen to go out there and win because her baseliner style isn't aggressive. She has to be prepared to keep on going in a match for however long it takes, she needs to be unbelievably keen and hungry.'

Sometimes that iron will to win, which has seemed so automatic in the past in the world's arch competitor, is stoked in a way which says a lot about the woman behind the champion. When Chris was playing in the Pretty Polly Classic in Brighton she was in serious danger of losing to rising Swedish star Catarina Lindqvist. She survived 6-2, 2-6, 7-6 and afterwards thanked a close girlfriend who had driven down from London to support her: "Thank you for coming; I think I gave a little more because I knew there was someone here for me."

John sees himself playing on for the foreseeable future. "I'm still enjoying it and I haven't had any hint yet of slowing down or going out on court and not wanting to play, or not wanting to train. I feel I've wasted three or four years when I totally let my tennis slip. Now I think I'm getting better and there are some things I can still achieve in the game. I'm only really getting into my second stage.'

John acknowledged that the problem of retirement is in proportion to their different levels in the game. 'It's a major decision which affects a champion of Chris's stature more than someone like me. It's very traumatic for athletes as they come to the end of their careers, having to decide when to stop and then coping with withdrawal symptoms afterwards. It wouldn't be nice to see a champion like Chris going down,' he said.

It's a measure of Chris's intelligent approach to retirement that she has eased herself into a transitional period over the last years, making plans to build up her involvement in the business side of the companies whose products she endorses. But more importantly, she has prepared herself mentally to look forward to the act of retiring and what new opportunities it will bring her: looking to the next phase of her life rather than seeing retirement as just laying down her racket.

'Now I'm beginning to feel that it's more normal to do everyday things than it is to play in tournaments. There's more pressure on me in tennis and sometimes I wonder why I am putting myself through it again. Until the last year or two I felt awkward when I had time off – I didn't know what to do with myself. After two days I was looking around and bored to tears. My *normal* life was going out on court, facing the pressure and being competitive; the abnormal one was taking time off. But I'm starting to enjoy my free time. I'm also starting to feel more of a businesswoman.

'Tennis has taken up a real chunk of my life and, as wonderful as it's been to me, I know that in a sense it's a shallow part of my life. I have begun to realize there are more meaningful things I can do. I've already had my chance of winning titles, and I've got all the money I'm going to need. Although it is still a thrill for me, how many times can you pat yourself on the back for winning a big tournament?

'I used to panic about retirement when I was younger because my happiness was based on whether I was winning or losing. If I was winning I was on top of the world. It was important at the time but looking back it was very superficial. I don't think I'll miss the pressure or the charge of adrenalin. I'll get pangs the first Wimbledon I'm not playing. I'll miss making a one hundred per cent commitment to something, but maybe I'll be able to commit myself to other things instead, including a family.

In fact, he didn't realise these ambitions but acquitted himself respectably in the singles by toughing out a match against thirteenth seed Eliot Teltscher in which he had to come back from being within two points of defeat.

He was deeply disappointed not to complete the mixed doubles hat-trick; John and Wendy went down to the Australian pair, John Fitzgerald and Elizabeth Smylie – who were the eventual runners up – in the quarter-finals.

John's finest hour came at the Australian Open where his 6–2, 1–6, 6–4, 6–7, 6–4 victory over seventh seed Joachim Nystrom of Sweden in the fourth round was his most spectacular win since his defeats of Henrik Sundstrom and Johan Kriek at Flushing Meadow in 1984.

John had arrived early in Melbourne and worked out with Stan Nicholes, the man who in 1982 had shocked John by telling him that he was at the point of no-return, and so had launched John's resurgence with an intensive training programme.

At Kooyong he disposed of the no. 11 seed, Tomas Smid of Czechoslovakia, and Jacob Hlasek of Switzerland before meeting Nystrom.

Ivan Lendl halted any further advance after that but John had made it to the quarter-finals for the first time since 1977 which propelled him up the rankings to finish the year at 42.

John's Davis Cup performance also won him acclaim. He was the veteran of the side against Israel in the European B Zone final, and found himself under considerable pressure at the start of Cup week in Eastbourne.

'I felt responsible for Britain having gone down the year before because I'd played poorly. This year was our chance to get back into the World Group but a lot of people were criticising Paul Hutchins because they felt this was the time to drop me and put in a young team and experiment.'

His fellow Davis Cup players were Jeremy Bates, Stephen Shaw, Stuart Bale and Colin Dowdeswell, but it was John's matches which were the crucial ones.

'If I'd lost either of those singles we would have stayed down and the headlines would have been: "Britain still can't get up into Division 2."' But, for the first time in twelve years of representing Britain in the Davis Cup, John won his three live rubbers – two singles and a doubles.

He inflicted defeat on Amos Mansdorf 14–12, 6–3, 4–6, 6–3 and with partner Colin Dowdeswell beat Shlomo Glickstein and Shahar Perkiss, but the climax was his tense and exciting 6–1, 6–1, 3–6, 6–3 victory over Shlomo Glickstein.

'It was a marvellous effort at precisely the time it was most needed,' John Parsons commented in the *Daily Telegraph*.

While John was playing his heart out to get Britain out of Davis Cup doldrums and promoted back into the World Group, Chris was making the faultless patriotic effort in the Wightman Cup audiences on both sides of the Atlantic have come to expect of her. In Williamsburg she beat Jo Durie and Annabel Croft to help America to a 7–0 victory, which meant that they retained the Cup for the seventh successive year and Chris pushed her own unbeaten singles record in thirteen years of playing Wightman Cup to a staggering twenty-six matches.

Chris and John's tally of triumphs nevertheless conceal fundamental questions about their futures, on and off court. How long does Chris want to go on playing full-time competitive tennis? What could replace the exhilaration of winning and all the adulation which is lavishly on her as a superstar? How do John and Chris envisage their lives after tennis?

'Personal relationships and friendships are more important to me now than they were before. If you're no. 1 in the world everybody's always coming up and patting you on the back, giving you attention, and sometimes you mistake that for people caring about you. It's really a myth about being happy when you're at the top and it's only afterwards that you realize that's not what life is really about.'

Whenever John and Chris choose to retire, and whether they do so at the same time or not, they will still have massive readjustments to make. The two twenty-four-year-old tennis players who married in 1979 will, as a retired couple in their thirties, have to carve out new jobs and settle down to the longer, post-tennis phase of their lives.

Over will be the gypsy-like living out of suitcases and racket bags, moving from country to country each week or fortnight – virtually the only existence they have known for all their adult years. But gone, too, will be the incentive of competition and the 'high' of winning. The adulation will diminish, the fame will fade; a new clutch of stars will succeed them as they once succeeded others. The autograph hunters will be less numerous and one day they'll even have to introduce themselves instead of always being recognized.

For the first time in their married lives they'll have to set up a permanent home and become accustomed to domesticity, a semblance of which has only entered their lives so far during the few weeks they spend in their Kingston house twice a year and their breaks in Palm Springs.

One of the important decisions they will have to make is where to settle. They bought their Palm Springs holiday home already decorated and furnished, and Mrs Evert did most of the decoration in Kingston, so it will be a novelty for them to do what most people start their married life with – the act of stamping their joint personalities on a home.

'John is English so we'll always have a base in London and hopefully spend the summers there rather than winters!' Chris said. 'We're still talking about where we'll have our base in the States; we've signed as touring pros for The Polo Club in Boca Raton, so we'll have a base near my family. We're leaning towards Los Angeles for a home – we have friends there and a couple of endorsements so it would be good for business. It sounds extravagant to have three homes but we can afford it.'

As the less outgoing and adventurous of the two, John has a

more relaxed approach as to how he'll occupy his time out of the game. He talks about the prospect more as retiring from the game, settling down to family life and slowing up.

By contrast Chris is a live-wire, bristling with enthusiasm to have a go at almost anything. For example, friends had difficulty dragging her out of the water once she had discovered snorkelling on Australia's Barrier Reef last year.

Already the endorsements she has take up a fair amount of her time, yet she is keen to give them still more, which must delight her sponsors – Ellesse clothes, Converse shoes, Wilson Rackets, Lipton's tea, Rolex, British Airways, Bovril, Cirrus Banking Systems, USA Vitamins and contracts in Japan.

She is a playing editor of *World Tennis* magazine and on TV enjoys a reputation in front of the cameras which would be the envy of many a professional actress. She can get a highly successful thirty-second television commercial 'in the can' in one take. She's keen, too, to try other methods of promotion: 'Wilson Rackets would love me to do clinics, showing the racket, talking about it and discussing my game. I'd also like to get more involved in the investment of my money. My father and my lawyer have done that for me so far. I haven't had time before but now whenever I come home Dad shows me a quarterly report of the income and a breakdown of how much of it comes from stocks and bonds and how much from property and other sources, so I'd like to take more of an interest in that.'

She is also involved with her For Seasons brand of natural skin-care products for the active, healthy, outdoor woman and it is characteristic of her that she would stay with 'Vera's', the make she has used for years, rather than accept an offer from one of the more famous cosmetic companies. 'The simple reason is that when I went to her I didn't have very good skin – it was dehydrated and dry – and after using her products it cleared up completely and is now in great shape,' Chris said.

She also hopes to be a continuing voice in tennis when she stops playing through an involvement with the Women's Tennis Association. 1986 is Chris's third consecutive term as elected President of the WTA, which Billie Jean King launched in 1973 as an instrument through which professional women players could develop and run their game. Since then, it has become a considerable organization which promotes and administers women's tennis worldwide. Chris has acquired a reputation as a conscientious and respected president, who not only fully supports many of Billie Jean's original ideals, but also works to ensure that the organization serves the younger players' needs.

'I share Billie Jean's thinking that sponsorship is very important because there won't be tournaments unless there are good sponsors who can put in a lot of money. It's also important that the players support the WTA; the top men haven't always supported the Association of Tennis Professionals which is why the male game is rather mixed up and not well co-ordinated.

'In the women's game we're very successful at putting on $150,000 tournaments for the top players, but we lack enough $75,000 tournaments for the middle players ranked 75 to 150 in the world. I would like to see everyone satisfied but that's hard in an organization with nearly two hundred members. I feel I can see further than my and the other top players' interests and can relate to players at the lower levels because my sister Jeanne was on the tour so I saw the problems and frustrations she experienced qualifying for tournaments.

Peggy Gossett is very quick to praise Chris's professional business-minded approach. 'She writes thank you letters to the tournaments she attends, and to the WTA's endorsees. When she talks in a meeting, everyone listens because she was a role model for so many players and carries so much weight and respect.'

At a more practical level Chris wants to pass on some of her experience to young players. 'In a couple of years' time John and I will be looking for an endorsement to be touring pros for a camp or tennis centre, where we will give clinics and have a house on the site. Our eventual dream is to have our own tennis camp. However, I wouldn't want to go from travelling all over the world to just a nine-to-five job being a tennis pro. I would like to do some one- or two-week camps. I love going home to Holiday Park and helping because I actually like teaching and coaching, but I don't want to do them for eight hours a day.'

John has given his future some thought. 'I'm not panicking but I'm concerned that I haven't yet pinpointed something which will get me out of bed each morning. I don't want to just drift but that's a danger since I have a tendency to be lazy.' He hopes to continue with competitive tennis, perhaps playing in over-35 events. 'I'd enjoy seven or eight tournaments a year on that circuit. And I'd love to utilize the experience I've gained and be Britain's Davis Cup captain.' He is enthusiastic about running a tennis school, perhaps linked to brother David's club and swopping young players for training programmes. Outside tennis, John is considering various options. As a movie fan the entertainment world offers possibilities. 'I'd like to try acting, but I don't think I'd be terribly good at it, so that leaves the production front. The problem with starting something entirely new though is that it would be just like going back to the qualifying rounds again.'

Both coming from large, close-knit families they would like children of their own. John's elder sister, Anne, is married to sportswriter Bob Hammond and they live in Leigh-on-Sea with their four children. David opened the highly successful David Lloyd Slazenger Racket Club at Heston, Middlesex, in 1982 and has opened a second club at Sutton. He and his wife Veronica have three children. Younger brother, Tony, whose competitive career was hampered by a back complaint, is head pro at David's club and married Gillian Storey in 1984.

John is in slightly more of a hurry to become a parent than Chris, although she was brought up to get married and have children. 'I think I'll just play one or two more years and have kids,' she has said with such regularity that it sounds like a tape recording.

By the time she had reached her late twenties she'd wrestled with the mental conflict of career versus full-time motherhood, and decided that the latter wasn't for her. The success her tennis has brought her has inevitably expanded her horizons and she has become a resourceful, competent, professional businesswoman, anxious to transfer her talents to other spheres: 'I really don't feel stimulated by the thought of just being a mother. Much as I respect my mother and Mrs Lloyd and women who have been homemakers, I've been a career girl my whole life and I don't think I could just stay at home.'

Both Lloyds are thoughtful enough not to want to start their family until they are certain about the quality of their mended marriage and know that they both have roughly the same vision of the future.

Their children, if and when they have them, won't be drilled to be tennis champions as soon as they can walk. 'It was hard enough for our brothers and sisters having to live with our success. I wouldn't envy our children. We're definitely not going to pressure them into playing tennis,' Chris said. 'There is no need to bring a child up like I was, and I think we'll introduce them to a lot of sports. John, for example, would love to see a boy play football.'

Chris worries that with the sort of area they'll live in and the life they'll lead on an eight-figure fortune, it will be difficult to bring children up with the sort of values and standards she adheres to. 'I dread the thought of poor little rich kids,' she said.

John is more confident: 'You've just got to be strict about things,' he said and Chris, who is nevertheless looking forward to parenthood, adds, 'I think I'm going to be a disciplined mother, but I'm always going to listen to my son or daughter.'

She would like to have a break between retiring from the rigours of the circuit and settling down. Ironically she wants to travel and see more of the very cities in which she has so often been confined to the airport, hotel and courts. 'I still have this fantasy about travelling, whether it's to India, Greece or Peru. That's what the money I've won will be useful for – not for inflating my ego but for providing me with the freedom to travel. I'd love to take John or Kathy or a friend and travel to all those places.'

John and Chris each have plans to take up other sports once their professional tennis careers are over. John would like to play golf, especially in Palm Springs. 'I love the idea of driving around eighteen holes at eight or nine in the morning with a couple of beers in the golf cart, but I don't want to get hooked until my tennis career's finished,' he said.

Chris will neither be caddying nor keeping him company on the greens. 'I just think golf might be a little slow,' she surmised after having tried nine holes once. Although she doesn't warm to the idea of swopping her racket for a set of clubs, skimming down ski slopes does appeal to her. 'I'd like to try skiing because coming from Florida where it's summer all year round it would be a completely different, new experience. I'd like the snow and getting close to nature, and the atmosphere.'

Nor is John likely to be sitting next to her on the chairlift. He thinks he's seen enough snow and slush in England to last him a lifetime.

But despite all the talk Chris still feels that the days of golf clubs and skis are some way off. 'Maybe my retirement instincts will surface in six months, maybe in two years,' she said.

When she does quit the game, women's tennis will be the poorer. By her example she has shown every professional player exactly how to behave on court – both in victory and defeat. She personifies the Kipling line which is engraved over the door to the Centre Court at Wimbledon, a door through which she has walked so many times: 'If you can meet with triumph and disaster and treat those two imposters just the same . . .'

In an era when some tennis players seem only to smash rackets and hurl obscenities, the general respect and admiration for Chris only increases. There is nothing but praise for her, from Melbourne to Miami, from taxi drivers to tennis pros. Tommy Tucker, the pro at Mission Hills Country Club in Palm Springs, has even dedicated one of the clay courts there to her 'for sportsmanship and style'. An American sporting magazine recognized her contribution by nominating her their 'Athlete of the Decade'.

But there is, at the same time, that other quality in her – that iron-hard determination to succeed or die in the trying. Not even the few failures she's had were for lack of trying. This quality is in everything she does – it was in her upbringing, in her rise to the top, in her epic battles with Tracy and Martina, even, ironically, in her marriage to John, and is certainly in her plans for the future.

As she walked back from the court after her momentous victory over Martina in Key Biscayne in Florida in January 1985, a friend said to her, 'Chris, you can retire now.' She paused, then replied, 'No, I want to go out on top.'

Fontana Paperbacks: Non-fiction

Fontana is a leading paperback publisher of non-fiction. Below are some recent titles.

☐ THE LIVING PLANET David Attenborough £8.95
☐ SCOTLAND'S STORY Tom Steel £4.95
☐ HOW TO SHOOT AN AMATEUR NATURALIST Gerald Durrell £2.25
☐ THE ENGLISHWOMAN'S HOUSE
                               Alvilde Lees-Milne and Derry Moore £7.95
☐ BRINGING UP CHILDREN ON YOUR OWN Liz McNeill Taylor £2.50
☐ WITNESS TO WAR Charles Clements £2.95
☐ IT AIN'T NECESSARILY SO Larry Adler £2.95
☐ BACK TO BASICS Mike Nathenson £2.95
☐ POPPY PARADE Arthur Marshall (ed.) £2.50
☐ LEITH'S COOKBOOK
                            Prudence Leith and Caroline Waldegrave £5.95
☐ HELP YOUR CHILD WITH MATHS Alan T. Graham £2.95
☐ TEACH YOUR CHILD TO READ Peter Young and Colin Tyre £2.95
☐ BEDSIDE SEX Richard Huggett £2.95
☐ GLEN BAXTER, HIS LIFE Glen Baxter £4.95
☐ LIFE'S RICH PAGEANT Arthur Marshall £2.50
☐ H FOR 'ENRY Henry Cooper £3.50
☐ THE SUPERWOMAN SYNDROME Marjorie Hansen Shaevitz £2.50
☐ THE HOUSE OF MITFORD Jonathan and Catherine Guinness £5.95
☐ ARLOTT ON CRICKET David Rayvern Allen (ed.) £3.50
☐ THE QUALITY OF MERCY William Shawcross £3.95
☐ AGATHA CHRISTIE Janet Morgan £3.50

You can buy Fontana paperbacks at your local bookshop or newsagent. Or you can order them from Fontana Paperbacks, Cash Sales Department, Box 29, Douglas, Isle of Man. Please send a cheque, postal or money order (not currency) worth the purchase price plus 15p per book for postage (maximum postage required is £3).

NAME (Block letters) _____

ADDRESS _____

_____

_____